Desktop Publishing With WordPerfect 6

Desktop Publishing With WordPerfect 6

Richard Mansfield

VENTANA
PRESS

Desktop Publishing With WordPerfect 6
Copyright © 1993 by Richard Mansfield

Library of Congress Cataloging-in-Publication Data

Mansfield, Richard.
    Desktop publishing with WordPerfect 6 / Richard Mansfield.
        p.   cm.
        Includes index.
        ISBN 1-56604-049-3
        1. WordPerfect (Computer file) 2. Desktop publishing
    I. Title.
    Z52.5.W65M24 1993
    686.2'2544536--dc20   93-21943
                        CIP

Book design: Karen Wysocki
Cover design: *Series concept:* Holly Russel; *adaptation:* Marcia Webb
Index service: Dianne Bertsch, Answers Plus
Technical review: Brian Little
Editorial staff: Marion Laird, Pam Richardson
Production staff: Liberated Types, Marcia Webb, Karen Wysocki
Proofreading: Eric Edstam

First Edition 9 8 7 6 5 4 3 2 1
Printed in the United States of America

Ventana Press, Inc.
P.O. Box 2468
Chapel Hill, NC 27515
919/942-0220
FAX 919/942-1140

Trademarks

Trademarked names appear throughout this book. Rather than list the names and entities that own the trademarks or insert a trademark symbol with each mention of the trademarked name, the publisher states that it is using the names only for editorial purposes and to the benefit of the trademark owner with no intention of infringing upon that trademark.

About the Author

Richard Mansfield's books have sold more than 250,000 copies worldwide. He was editor-in-chief of *COMPUTE!* magazine for seven years. His published work includes columns on computer topics, magazine articles and several short stories. He is the author of *Machine Language for Beginners*, *WordPerfect Macro Solutions*, *The Visual Guide to Visual Basic* (also published by Ventana Press) and eight other computer books. He is currently a full-time writer.

Acknowledgments

My gratitude for their talents goes to the gifted staff at Ventana Press—these people care about books. I must single out Marion Laird for her sensitive, thoughtful editing; she responds to writing with care and latitude. Thanks to Karen Wysocki for her excellent design sense. For her kindness and refined diplomatic skills, Pam Richardson merits special mention. For their overview, foresight and dedication to quality, Elizabeth and Joe Woodman, the founders and guiding hands of Ventana Press.

I would also like to thank my mother for encouraging me to combine textual and visual aesthetics (and for being encouraging no matter what); my brother John for teaching me how morality is intimately related to effort; Jim Coward for his constancy and highly developed, civilized appreciation of books and art; Larry O'Connor for exemplifying gentle, hopeful, artistic work; Dr. MackSoud for demonstrating commitment and describing relativity; Dr. Stuurman for showing me many things I could not see; Robert Lock for supplying a perspective I had never, would never have, considered; Kathleen Martinek for her enlightened humanity; and David Lee Roach for demonstrating how noble struggle can be.

Dedication

For Larry

Contents

Introduction

With Version 6.0, WordPerfect has now joined a select group of computer programs that can turn out publications of the highest professional quality.

In this book I've tried to accomplish two goals: To show how to get the most out of WordPerfect 6.0's many desktop publishing features and to demonstrate the techniques and trends of effective contemporary design.

Whether you're in charge of publishing a small club newsletter or preparing materials for a major corporate ad campaign, WordPerfect 6.0 has the tools to produce first-class results for all types of publications. I've tried to show you how to use those tools to maximum effect.

The other half of the publishing task—effective design—is often taught in classes and books as a set of rules. But I agree with those who say there really are no rules. Instead of rules, I've filled this book with examples. The purpose of these examples is to get you to experiment—relying on and, I hope, amplifying your personal creativity and sense of style. The only absolute rule I've learned in many years of publishing is that, in fact, there are no *laws* of design—merely trends.

There are no ironclad rules.

HOW TO USE THIS BOOK

This is a book of suggestions, guidelines and examples, not a book of *rules*. Ultimately, there are no rules in design. Fashions come and go; what looks good this year might have been laughed at last year, or will be thought laughable next year. (Remember razor-thin belts and beehive hairdos?)

What's more, good design for a corporate proposal is likely to be bad design for an advertisement. So, rather than learning rules, most of which are only temporary, it's better to learn to *look* critically. To discover ways to think about the qualities of a page you're designing. And above all to let yourself be imaginative, creative, even playful.

ALMOST EFFORTLESS GRAPHIC DESIGN

Powerful and highly visual, WordPerfect 6.0 makes it easy to try out various approaches quickly and with little effort. And once you learn what to look for when arranging text and illustrations on a page, you can make your publications more attractive and effective. It's this kind of looking and thinking that this book encourages you to explore.

WHAT'S IN THIS BOOK?

✔ Chapter 1 introduces you to some of WordPerfect 6.0's new features. It covers the value and purposes of good design. It also includes a brief history of desktop publishing (DTP) and the parallel development of WordPerfect into the dynamic DTP engine it has become.

✔ Chapter 2 explains several ways to get started on a design; then, through examples, shows you how to balance the large elements—text blocks, headlines and graphic elements.

✔ Chapter 3 goes into detail about typefaces, spacing and other, more subtle typographical refinements. If the large elements are comparable to the *shape* and the *color* of a suit of clothes, these smaller elements are like the *texture*. Perhaps not crucial—but important nonetheless.

✔ Chapter 4 moves out from the details to the middle ground—how to improve your publications by manipulating margins, columns, text alignment and lines, and adding special effects such as shadowing.

✔ In Chapter 5, we look at the pitfalls, the flaws you should check for when you've finished your page designs and are ready to publish. Many common design problems—from crowding to supersymmetry—are illustrated with before-and-after examples. In this chapter you learn techniques that allow you to take a truly objective look at your work.

✔ Chapter 6 shows you how to use styles, macros, keyboards and button bars to automate and simplify common desktop publishing tasks. Several useful DTP macros and styles are described, and you'll learn, step by step, how to add them to your WordPerfect toolkit.

✔ Chapter 7 explores several of WordPerfect 6.0's most useful DTP features: how to get the most out of WP's Text and Image Editors, and how to insert and modify watermarks, borders, lines and captions.

✔ Chapter 8, like Chapter 5, is filled with before-and-after examples, called *makeovers* in the trade, that include logos, fax cover sheets, stationery, advertisements, newsletters, menus and more. The idea in showing these makeovers is that no design is ever completely bad or altogether perfect. You can look at almost any page design and make it better—with knowledge, practice, persistence and a bit of luck. This book endeavors to give you the knowledge and some of the practice. The persistence and luck are up to you.

WHAT YOU NEED TO GET STARTED

Because WordPerfect is marvelously adaptable to each user's needs and preferences, it includes many ways to achieve a goal. It also works with many configurations of equipment—from older, slower computers to the latest 486 screamer. But here are some suggestions that will likely save you some time if you are planning to use WordPerfect 6.0 for more than casual, occasional desktop publishing.

Consider getting a mouse if you don't have one.

✔ First, use a mouse. Many people object to mice, but there's nothing better for many graphics tasks, such as moving or resizing an illustration. What takes dozens of keystrokes and five menu-submenu maneuvers via the keyboard takes only a click with the mouse. You don't have to use the mouse for text editing or menu access—WP lets you take either the keyboard or the mouse route. But for making adjustments to graphics, there really is no comparison.

✔ Try to use as powerful a PC as possible. The faster your processor (386 or 486 recommended), the more quickly the screen will redraw when you move a Graphics Box, change a headline, or even bring down a menu. Graphics take lots of computer power and WP's new Graphics and Page Views are excellent for designing. But on older machines the slow redraw will eventually annoy you. For these same reasons, try to add as much internal memory to your computer as you can afford.

Use Graphics Mode when designing.

✔ Try to purchase as large a color monitor as possible. The less WP has to shrink a page to show you the whole page onscreen, the more detail you'll see when you're looking critically at your work.

✔ Stay in Graphics Mode (instead of Page, or Text, Mode) when designing. For reasons explained in Chapter 1, WP's new Graphics Mode is superior to the alternatives when you are editing your page design.

come up with an imaginative and you're enjoying yourself. In other words, relax! There are no rules that can't be broken.

Let's get started.

The Extinction
1 of the Dinosaurs

WordPerfect, the world's most popular word processor, has now become a powerful desktop publishing engine. With the release of Version 6.0, WP is as *visual* as a PC program can get. It joins GeoWorks and a select group of other DOS-based programs that look as good onscreen *graphically* as Windows and the Macintosh.

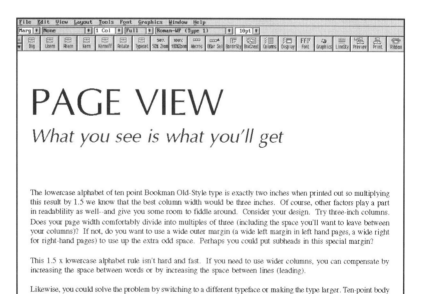

Figure 1-1: When you edit or design in WordPerfect 6.0, you see exactly what the printed results will look like.

Font installation and "watermarks" are two of WordPerfect's many desktop publishing features.

However, WP 6.0 isn't merely good-looking. Many of its new features contribute to effective desktop publishing. There's an Image Editor you can use to rotate photos and drawings (to *any* of 360 degrees), adjust brightness and contrast and manipulate images in many other ways.

WP's Font Installer allows you to add hundreds of inexpensive typefaces. There's a "watermark" feature which allows you to superimpose text on top of graphics. In fact, if there's a tool that will help you to create truly professional-looking newsletters, business forms, advertisements, catalogs, flyers and other publications, WordPerfect is likely to offer it in Version 6.0.

VERSION 6 GOES VISUAL

Above all, Version 6.0 is highly visual: you *see* on the screen the effect of changing the size of a headline or moving a drawing. If you have a mouse, you can drag a photo around the screen "page" as easily as you could slide a photo around on top of your desk. You can resize a graphic in seconds by just dragging one of its corners. In other words, WP 6.0 has all the facilities you could want when designing most kinds of documents.

If you can think it up, WordPerfect 6.0 can probably do it. For example, you can create custom borders to frame photos, drawings or text. You can *design* a border from scratch, specifying line thickness, pattern, color, shade—even rounding off the corners. You can add shadows and superimposed elements that give your pages depth and strength by utilizing these and other sophisticated design techniques.

Figure 1-2: **Before:** If you don't like a design . . .

Figure 1-3: **After:** . . . you can easily resize and reposition text, headlines and graphics.

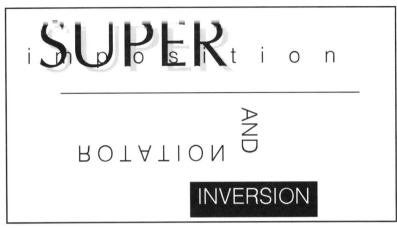

Figure 1-4: Using WP 6.0's improved graphics features—superimposition, rotation and inversion—couldn't be simpler.

WHY BOTHER TO DESIGN?

Designing a publication takes more time than simply typing it. So, why bother to design? What's the advantage of adding a headline, a border, a photo or other special effects to a printed page? After all, until recently most companies (and virtually all individuals) communicated by typing, or even handwriting, their newsletters and other publications.

If a company wanted to reach a large audience *and impress that audience*, it hired an ad agency and spent thousands of dollars to have professionals create a "look." But for instruction manuals and other in-house training materials, memos, proposals, reports and most other communications, simple typing was good enough. The alternative—a designed page—was too time-consuming and expensive.

Personal computers have changed all that; professional
design tools are now available to ~~... ... ...~~

~~... ...~~ designed
page is more
convincing to
the reader.

more attractive. Consequently, more people will actually *read*
what you publish. And, having read it, if it's handsomely
designed, more people will believe what it says.

Whether you're printing a business advertisement for the
want-ads page, a set of name badges or a church bulletin,
anything you publish will look more attractive, more professional and more *believable* if you take a little extra time to design it. Just as you would be less convincing if you asked
your boss for a raise wearing a soiled T-shirt, publications
that *look* bad have less impact than those that look good. It
almost doesn't matter what your publication says if its design
is thoughtless, plain or amateurish.

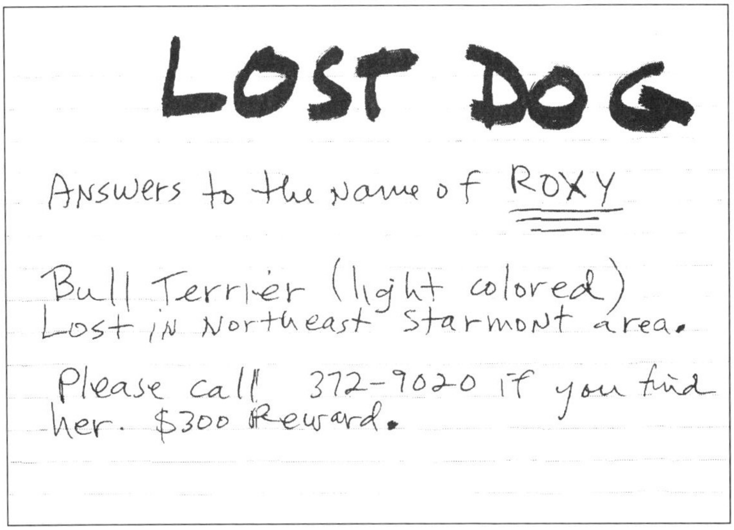

Figure 1-5: Passing the bulletin board in your grocery store, would
you be more likely to notice this item . . .

Figure 1-6: . . . or this one?

GETTING RESULTS

When you publish something, you usually want results. You want people to be attracted to it, to read it and, finally, to act on it. Consider the example illustrated in Figures 1-5 and 1-6: your beloved Roxy chewed right through the fence and ran away. So you decide to print 50 copies of a Lost Dog ad and

Figure 1-6 have become widely available and relatively inexpensive. You already have a computer and WordPerfect 6.0. The only other tool required to create Figure 1-6 is a $150 scanner (a small wand that you pass over a photo or drawing to bring the image into the computer as a graphics file).

However, less than a decade ago, you would have had to hire a professional designer, typesetter and printing firm to produce this ad. And the equipment necessary to print documents containing shadowing, proportional type, headlines and photos would have cost you hundreds of thousands of dollars. No wonder most written communication used to originate from the typewriter and the human hand.

THE EXTINCTION OF THE DINOSAURS

In the late 1970s, I went into a large Salvation Army store. Behind the stacks of mattresses, racks of clothes and boxes of chipped china was a room containing several huge machines. I didn't know it at the time, but these machines were not merely broken or used—they were obsolete.

One was a punch card sorting machine the size of a pickup truck. A notice attached to it claimed that it had cost a bank $250,000 and was now being offered for $700. It seemed like a bargain. After all, those punch cards were still widely used. Do you remember them? They always said, "Do not fold, spindle or mutilate," although nobody knew exactly what *spindle* meant.

Also in this room was a "memory" for a mainframe computer—hundreds of metal tokens suspended in a matrix of piano wire. Gathering dust nearby was an accountant's immense mechanical "calculating engine." Unlike the ordinary hand-cranked adding machines of the day, this engine could *multiply and divide*. And in the back, still oiled and gleaming, was a linotype machine for $1,200. I hope nobody bought the

If it weighs more than 100 pounds, don't buy it.

linotype. Within a few years, these machines would become as useless as the bank's card-sorter. During the 1960s and 1970s, handsetting of metal type was being replaced by a process called *phototypesetting*, which was a precursor to laser printing. Today, even phototypesetting is virtually dead. Almost all magazines and newspapers are now designed on desktop systems just like the one you use.

THE END OF THE AGE OF HEAVY METAL

Just as giant reptiles gave way to tiny rodents at the end of the age of dinosaurs, heavy equipment has now given way to the personal computer. A linotype machine was a keyboard attached to a small *foundry*. A typesetter would sit at the machine and type in a line of text. The lino would then pour hot metal into a form. After the letters of the text had hardened, the "slugs" were slathered with printer's ink, and magazine or newspaper pages could then be pounded out. Similar techniques involving hot lead produced the illustrations and headlines too.

Now graphics and text are stored in computer memory. Information inside a computer or on a disk is a pattern of electromagnetic fields; it is stored there in much the same way information is stored in the human brain. (In the brain, the fields are highly efficient, very low-power, and, of course, wet. Computer memory is made of silicon, the same material as glass and sand. The brain is a type of "meat." But the idea's the same.)

No longer do text and illustrations have to be molded in metal (or, more recently, made into a photographic negative) before a page can be printed. Instead, electronic pulses travel through a cable to a printer where the information is then stamped, burned or sprayed onto the page.

Because we've now got the lead out of the process, today millions of people can *design* their own communications.

THE EVOLUTION OF WORDPERFECT

...... machines to create italics, enlarge characters for a headline, and otherwise manipulate the attributes of text and graphics. A typical code might look like this: [Itk;)24RO], specifying the type size, typeface and the fact that italics were being turned on at this point in the text.

Most of the early word processors merely aped this process. If you wanted [Itk;)12RO]*italics*[Itn;)12RO] you had to type in the code or, sometimes, select italics from a menu, and the codes were inserted for you. But what was truly ugly about all this was that onscreen you could see dozens of these codes mixed in with the actual text.

One of the primary reasons for WordPerfect's huge success is that those codes were hidden from the writer. You could see them if you wanted to (in code view), but otherwise you had a screen as clean as typing paper.

For several years, though, even in WordPerfect, you had to print out a copy of a page to see what the final result would look like. "Text View" was all there was, although when color came to computer screens, WP used color to indicate various appearance attributes, such as italic and bold, in the text. But you still couldn't see on your screen the actual graphics, type sizes or text attributes as they would look when they were printed out.

> WordPerfect's first great feature was a clean screen page.

PRINT PREVIEW ARRIVES

Then, when computers with enough memory and speed to handle graphics became available, WordPerfect introduced "Print Preview," which allowed you to see onscreen an imitation of how the printed page would look. You still couldn't *do* anything to the text or graphics in Print Preview—you had to go back to Text View (sometimes called Edit View) to make any adjustments to your document. Nevertheless, Print Preview saved a lot of paper and a lot of time.

When you make a headline larger or smaller, for example, you want to see the effect it has on how the entire page looks. Print Preview was a relatively convenient way to design. You at least didn't have to wait for the printer to show you what you'd done.

With WP 6.0, you can do what you want and see what you did.

Now, with WordPerfect 6.0, the final barrier has been crossed. You can freely edit and manipulate the text and graphics in a WYSIWYG (what-you-see-is-what-you-get) view. Text View is still there; and if you use an older, slower computer, Text View is still a good place to type or edit text. Changes show up instantly in Text View no matter how slow your computer is. With text, there's comparatively little information for the computer to manipulate. (A letter *a* takes up a single byte of computer memory; a photographic image can take up *four million bytes* or more.)

However, if you have a fast computer (386 or 486) and enough memory, you need never leave the new Graphics Modes: Page View and Graphics View. No matter what kind of computer you have, when you are arranging headlines, boxes, graphics or other elements of page design, nothing beats seeing your changes as you make them.

GRAPHICS VERSUS PAGE MODE

The distinction between WP's new Page and Graphics Modes is relatively minor. In both you'll see the typefaces, type sizes, attributes, photos and drawings as they'll appear when printed.

The difference is that Graphics Mode doesn't display footers, footnotes, headers or endnotes. It also doesn't show the top and bottom margins of the page. (Eliminating these margins has the effect of widening the page onscreen because WP stretches the image so the text and graphics remain undistorted.) In practice, this means that Graphics View is the better choice for most editing and design purposes. You have a larger surface on which to work.

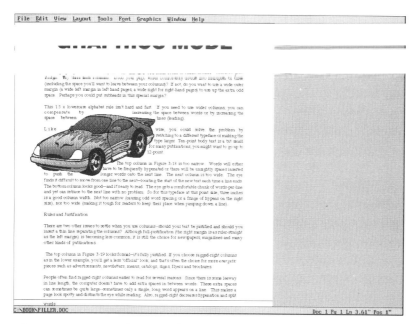

Figure 1-7: In Graphics Mode, top and bottom margins are reduced, giving you a larger viewing area for text and graphics.

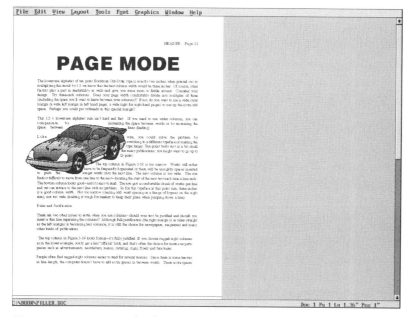

Figure 1-8: Page Mode shows exactly how a page will look when it's printed.

Page Mode for an exact copy; Graphics Mode for editing and designing.

Because Graphics View doesn't display full margins, text characters are a bit larger onscreen and therefore somewhat easier to read than they are in Page View. But WordPerfect 6.0 is almost always extremely flexible and customizable. There are many levels of *zoom* in both graphics viewing modes. When you want to see an *exact* replication of your page, switch to Page View or Print Preview.

MOVING ON

Now that we've surveyed some of the high points of WordPerfect's desktop publishing features, it's time to start designing pages. Only five or six years ago, that would have meant heating beeswax to paste sections of text and graphics onto "boards" (white cardboard page forms), setting out pencils and paint pots, and locating the Exacto knife. Instead, we'll just fire up WordPerfect 6.0.

In the next chapter, we'll consider the large elements of a page: headlines, boxes, borders, illustrations, blocks of text, and the white space which contains them all. Our main goal will be to learn to balance a page by moving and resizing the various zones of black, white and gray.

2 Creating the "Look"

There are many ways to make a publication attractive and inviting to the reader. The primary tools are headlines, white space, the typefaces you select for your text, and various kinds of illustrations. Where you place them on the page (and the size you make them) has a major impact on the visual appeal of your piece. Use these tools effectively and you're more than halfway to creating a successful, good-looking publication.

The other half of the task is roughly equivalent to what *editing* does for an article: you polish your design. You look at your pages—preferably after putting them aside for a few days. Then you look at them with a cold, objective eye. And you check to see that you've got balance, contrast, variety and so on. You also check the details: such flaws as crowding, hidden or floating headlines, "tombstones" (parallel headlines in adjacent columns), "widows" and "orphans" (stranded lines or fragments of text). In Chapter 4, we'll go through all the things you should double-check during this important second look at your work. For now, let's take a tour of the main approaches to creating a solid, attractive desktop publication.

Put your work aside for a while, then give it a cold look.

THINK LIKE AN ARTIST

One good way to start designing your publication is to pretend that you are about to paint an abstract painting in the style of Mondrian. One of the most influential 20th century artists, Piet Mondrian arranged squares and rectangles in attractive, balanced compositions. You've got a similar task. You have gray blocks of text, black blocks of headlines, perhaps some in-between shades of graphics, photos or charts.

Finally, to glue it all together, there's *white space*—the spaces where there's nothing but blank paper. Of all these elements, maybe the most important is the white space.

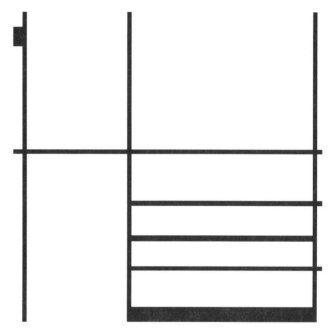

Figure 2-1: Mondrian created balanced, attractive designs out of rectangles.

Notice how the lines and white spaces *balance* in Figure 2-1. The shapes are distributed on the page so that no part of the page dominates the others. To see how it would look out of balance, put a white piece of paper on top of the little square in the top left. Do you see how the whole page is now dominated by the lower right? How the page sinks to the right and down? If this page were a white square plate and the text were lead, the whole thing would tilt to the lower right corner without that little square.

Clearly, balance isn't just a matter of comparing how much

black square emphasized by lots of white space, with the background. [illegible]

enough power to hold the page together. So when you design a page, you might want to first take a pencil and paper and sketch in the main elements. Roughly draw in rectangles for the page elements that you must include—the necessary text, etc. Then consider what's optional. Make a headline extra-large to balance something lower on the page. Or include a photo. You can play around with the positions of various things, and the margins of white around them, until you get a page that looks right—a page that doesn't tilt.

Fortunately, design isn't a puzzle with only one answer—there are many ways to put together a good page. But to make your publication look its best, think about where you put things and how large you make them.

Another experiment: cover up the little nubs, where the horizontal lines extend, along the right side of Figure 2-1. Do you see the weight of the page shift to the left as the eye is drawn to that powerful little black box? Yet another experiment: turn this book one quarter-turn to the right, so the black box is at the top. Does it still balance? Turn it another quarter-turn, then another, then another. It seems that Mondrian's design is balanced no matter how it's positioned, don't you think? Try this four-turns look at your own work—it's another good test of balance.

WHITE SPACE

White space is the background—the zones on the page where no text, headlines or graphics are placed. But in the past, white space wasn't considered a desirable page-design element. Margins around the sides of the pages were usually small, and text took up nearly the whole page. Any blank space was filled with designs and fancy borders. For one thing, paper was expensive and the designers didn't want to waste it. (As a result, designers didn't have to worry so much about balance because the pages contained less contrast.)

There are many ways to create a strong design.

Figure 2-2: In the past, pages were filled with text or designs. There was less use of white space.

While not necessarily unattractive, fully filled pages are not the current fashion. The busy and lacy borders shown in Figure 2-2 have largely disappeared from contemporary publications.

Today, the reader expects smaller units of text, separated by white—places where the eye can relax. White space also allows you to organize the text and graphics logically—to emphasize certain areas of text and to subordinate others.

Figure 2-3: The boxed text on the right is a "sidebar"; it's related to the main text, but reading it is optional.

A wide margin is also a good place to put summarizing text that tags and defines or explains the body text (somewhat like handwritten notes in the margins of a book). This way, the reader can skim your publication, moving from one summary to the next, to find subjects of interest.

By using a wide margin, your pages will have a more "open," less formidable look than the wall-to-wall gray of a page filled with text.

White space is an important element of contemporary design.

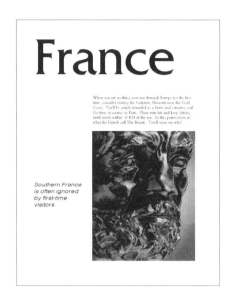

France

When you are working your way through Europe for the first time, consider visiting the Sculpture Museum near the Gold Coast. You'll be amply rewarded as a brave and cunning soul. Go first, of course, to Paris. Then turn left and keep driving until you're within 30 KM of the sea. At this point you're in what the French call The Beauty. You'll soon see why!

*Southern France
is often ignored
by first-time
visitors*

**Pull-quotes
seduce your
readers.**

Figure 2-4: Here's one way to add white space and give more "air" to a page.

Such summaries can be in the form of subheads (smaller headlines than the main article headline) or brief one- or two-sentence descriptions. Another kind of margin summary is the *pull-quote*, a sentence or short segment "pulled" directly from the main text of an article. Magazines typically try to entice the reader by selecting several interesting or sensational sentences as pull-quotes. Other types of publications, such as newsletters, corporate documents or more formal pieces, may simply use a summary that describes the adjacent text.

When your publication is longer than a single page, the reader will normally be viewing two pages at the same time.

Two pages taken as a unit are called a *spread*, and you will

spread. The top and bottom margins should be the same for

margin should be made wide on the right page to match.

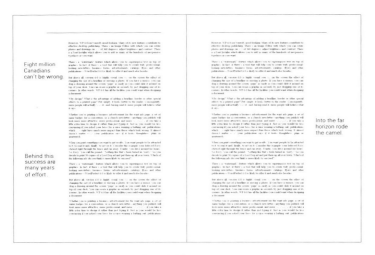

Figure 2-5: Facing pages should have symmetrical margins.

HEADLINES & SUBHEADS

Think of headlines as your darkest, heaviest page design features. They are usually the first text elements on the page to be read and among the first graphic elements to be noticed. Put headlines in an awkward place or make them too big or too small and a page is thrown off balance.

The main headline is usually placed near the top of a page and is set in type considerably bigger than the text, the "body text." (Sometimes you won't use subheads, so the main headline will be the only headline.)

Figure 2-6: Avoid making your headlines so small that they get lost in the body of the text.

Headlines in sans, body text in serif: a rule not often broken.

Contemporary design has settled on a convention: the body text is set in a serif font and the headlines in sans-serif. *Serifs* are the little extra jots and curlicues at the ends of the strokes that make up the character's design. Technically, *font* means the typeface (such as "Swiss"), the style (such as "italic"), and the size. However, in this book we're going to use the terms *typeface* and *font* interchangeably.

SANS-SERIE A MODERN- LOOKING TYPEFACE

Serif Typefaces Convey A More Traditional Feeling

Figure 2-7: The characters in a *serif* typeface (like Times Roman) are more varied in shape and size than characters in sans-serif typefaces (such as Univers or Helvetica).

The letters in a serif font are easier for the eye to distinguish—they make body text easier to read.

Sans-serif characters are more modern-looking. In fact, sans-serif fonts did not appear until the 19th century. Before that, all characters (except in some Greek typefaces) included the little flourishes and curls, the legacy of hand-lettered manuscripts produced by countless scribes, clerks, and monks over the years.

However, the old rule that you should only use sans-serif typefaces in titles and headlines is yielding now to a trend that occasionally permits serif faces. The *New York Times* mostly uses Times Roman, a serif font, for its heads. Try setting them both ways and look at the results on the screen, using WordPerfect's Print Preview feature. Then decide which typeface style conveys the look that best suits the nature of your publication.

This Headline Tries to Convey Far Too Much Information and Thus Should Be Shortened

Put the cursor between them—we're going to Advance the second F up. To move the second F up, press Shift-F8, 7, 6, 4 to get to the "Advance, Up from Cursor" and type in .11 as the vertical lift.

How did we know to type in .11 as the vertical movement? It's just hit and miss—try a few different numbers until the logo looks right to you. Fortunately, WP6, with its highly visual Views, makes this kind of experimentation easier than it would be in Text View.

The easiest way to create a logo based on a company's initials in WP is to use the Advance feature. Advance allows you to position letters with great precision. Here's how we created Figure 8-3. Select the typeface by pressing Ctrl-F8, F. Then move with the arrow keys to select "Helve-WP Bold" and press Enter, S. Now type in 42 as the type size and press Enter Enter to get back to document view.

Put the cursor between them—we're going to Advance the second F up. To move the second F up, press Shift-F8, 7, 6, 4 to get to the "Advance, Up from Cursor" and type in .11 as the vertical lift.

How did we know to type in .11 as the vertical movement? It's just hit and miss—try a few different numbers until the logo looks right to you. Fortunately, WP6, with its highly visual Views, makes this kind of experimentation easier than it would be in Text View.

Put the cursor between them—we're going to Advance the second F up. To move the second F up, press Shift-F8, 7, 6, 4 to get to the "Advance, Up from Cursor" and type in .11 as the vertical lift.

How did we know to type in .11 as the vertical movement? It's just hit and miss—try a few different numbers until the logo looks right.

Forming Opinions

The easiest way to create a logo based on a company's initials in WP is to use the Advance feature. Advance allows you to position letters with great precision. Here's how we created Figure 8-3. Select the typeface by pressing Ctrl-F8, F. Then move with the arrow keys to select "Helve-WP Bold" and press Enter, S. Now type in 42 as the type size and press Enter Enter to get back to document view.

Put the cursor between them—we're going to Advance the second F up. To move the second F up, press Shift-F8, 7, 6, 4 to get to the "Advance, Up from Cursor" and type in .11 as the vertical lift.

How did we know to type in .11 as the vertical movement? It's just hit and miss—try a few different numbers until the logo looks right to you. Fortunately, WP6, with its highly visual Views, makes this kind of experimentation easier than it would be in Text View.

Figure 2-8: Try to keep headlines short, simple and direct.

*U*se inverted triangles for uneven headlines.

Since they are supposed to attract and quickly inform the reader, headlines should be short. But if your headline is too long to fit on a single line, use initial caps (capitalize only the first letter of each word) rather than all uppercase letters. And don't use an initial capital in short prepositions, conjunctions or articles *(in, to, a, and, an, or, the)* unless one of these short words is the first word in the headline.

When you create headlines, your goal should be to make all the lines approximately equal in length. If that's not possible, make the upper line longer than lower lines (to produce an inverted triangle shape). Use all-caps for short headlines, but initial capitals and lowercase for longer headlines. This maintains readability.

Secondary headlines (subheads) can be placed at appropriate intervals within the text. Subheads allow the reader to scan the text, reading only those sections that are of interest. Subheads also provide a quick way to get across the main points of an article. And, visually, they break up the masses of gray text with darker, bolder, larger type.

It's generally good practice to provide some white space above subheads (see Figure 2-8). This extra [...]

Figure 2-8 we've not only added extra space, we put in a *rule* (a line) to even more forcefully separate the subhead from the preceding text. Alternatively, you can place subheads in a margin. In either case, be sure that it's *visually* clear what section of the text the subhead belongs to. Readers resent unnecessary puzzles. Useless ambiguities in your design will cause your readers to think you have been sloppy, which indeed you have.

BULLETS, DINGBATS & ICONS

White space is the absence of text or graphics. White space is zones of light within a page. Text is zones of gray. Headlines are huge black text lines, letters blown up so much that they become dark design elements in themselves. Now we'll explore a hybrid element, something halfway between text and graphics, halfway between white and black.

A TREND TOWARD VISUALS

One of the most profound shifts in communication has been away from text and toward visuals. Clearly, movies and television have had a major impact on the way people prefer to absorb information. In the past few years, additional shifts have occurred, induced by television's expectation of a short attention span and the popular preference for *seeing* rather than *reading*. Icons—small symbolic pictures—are relatively new to page design and derive from three separate influences: MTV, *USA Today* and a growing enthusiasm among computer users for machines and software using a graphical user interface (GUI) like Windows and the Mac.

MTV and its journalistic equivalent, *USA Today*, have had a profound impact on both print and television design styles in the past decade. MTV and *USA Today* both break their information into small, rapidly identifiable, easily assimilated, highly *visual* units. This style is to reading what dim sum, shish kabob, tapas and sushi are to eating—most cuisines

Bullets, dingbats and icons are small, but they're useful in balancing a page.

Television has influenced almost all publication design styles.

have examples of meals composed of bite-sized portions. This was traditionally considered the *appetizer* phase of a dinner, but it's increasingly becoming the dinner itself. There is, in other words, no main course at all.

The *New York Times*, by contrast, will print *the entire speech* when the president addresses the congress. *USA Today* will print a bulleted list of the "highlights," and may include some icons (such as a stack of dollars for the paragraph on the economy, a Band-Aid for health issues, etc.).

The *Times* has no color, few stories, few symbols and relatively few photos. *USA Today*, by contrast, is filled with small bulleted lists, graphic symbols, many short items and much color. The emphasis is still shifting toward visuals and away from text. Nobody expects newspapers to end up with the 8-to-1 ratio of words to illustrations typical of comic books—but the trend toward graphics at the expense of words is not over yet.

The Macintosh computer and Windows software frequently use icons to stand for programs or features or for actions the computer user should take. The user clicks on an icon—for instance, a small picture of a disk—and the files on a disk drive are displayed. In page design, icons can symbolize a recurring interruption such as a summary, a caution or a helpful hint. They can also symbolize a regularly recurring feature or "department" of a newspaper or magazine—for example, a lightning bolt for the weather summary.

My local newspaper, The *Greensboro News & Record*, has taken iconization to an extreme. *Every* main subhead—there are perhaps a half-dozen per page—has a little silhouette of a clock face next to it. When the paper underwent its most recent redesign and added this strange feature, it was explained that these little clocks would let readers know: *here is a quick summary of this story*. (The clock icon supposedly alerts you that this is a time-saver. But when they are all over each page like roaches, who's saving time?) Like anything else, icons used too much become self-defeating and, let's be honest, silly. Since icons are crude pictures, they will attract the

The *New York Times* remains true to tradition.

Icons can get out of hand if you use them everywhere.

eye. If you want to put a dozen attractors on a page, consider
using the smaller bullets or some...

Small Pictures and Markers

Bullets are dots or squares (or sometimes other simple geometric designs such as diamonds). *Dingbats* are character-
sized pictures, line drawings of tiny stars, daggers, silhouettes of airplanes (there are hundreds of dingbats and they
come in sets). *Icons* are like dingbats, but they're usually
larger and contain more detail. Where bullets and dingbats
are often used to illustrate each small item in a list, icons are
generally used to symbolically identify the contents of whole
paragraphs or pages.

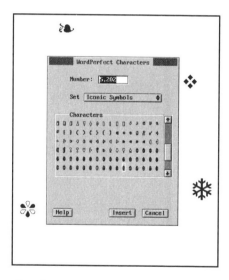

Figure 2-9: WordPerfect 6.0 contains a nice assortment of bullets
and dingbats.

You can quickly insert bullets and dingbats—a set of each
is supplied with WP. Just press Ctrl+W and you'll see a
menu. You'll find most of the bullets in "Character Map 4
(Typographic Symbols)," and the dingbats are in "Character
Map 5 (Iconic Symbols)." The Iconic Symbols are the Zapf
set, the most widely used collection of dingbats.

Special Note: Not all printers can print these special half graphic characters. To find out if your printer will reproduce all, some or none of the typographic and iconic symbols, load the file CHARACTR.TST, which comes with WP. Then print out the sets of characters to see what your printer does.

However, even if your printer will produce dingbats and icons, they might not show up on your monitor. If you're in WordPerfect 6.0's Text View (Ctrl+F3, 2), all you'll see is a square when you insert a bullet or dingbat. If you switch to WP's Page or Graphics View (Ctrl+F3, 3 or 4), you might or might not see the actual shape of the special symbols.

See what your printer can do with the file "CHARACTR.TST."

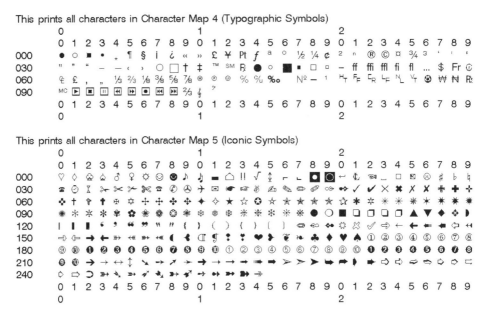

Figure 2-10: WordPerfect's sets of bullet and dingbat characters.

Figure 2-10 shows you a sample of what you'll see if you print out the file "CHARACTR.TST." When you press Ctrl+W to access the special characters, you could type in the code number for the character you want. Those numbers on top and to the left of the set of characters tell you which code to type in. For example, to insert the symbol for *male*, you would locate it in Character Map 5, the fifth item from the left. You would type in the character map number (5), a comma, then the character number (4). You add the number of the row (00) to the number of the character handy keep a copy of bullets and dingbats, you'll have to and use it to look up the proper codes.

If your screen will show the dingbats and bullets, you can select a character by using the arrow keys. Open the character window with Ctrl+W, then press Tab, 2, I (to select "Iconic Symbols"), then 3 to move into the character box. Now use the arrow keys to move over to the fourth character, the male circle-arrow symbol. If you have a mouse, just double-click on the character you want to insert.

When you have a list of short items, bullets are useful to alert the reader that this *is* a list and, further, that each of the items in the list is of roughly equal importance.

> B ullets say to the reader: This is a list.

- ✔ Use bullets to visually identify that the associated text is a list.

- ✔ Use dingbats in place of bullets for greater emphasis.

- ✔ Use icons to "list" whole paragraphs or to symbolize meaning.

```
┌─────────────────────────────┐
│                             │
│      Dottie F. Rebate       │
│     2233 Slow Clue Ln.      │
│     Bad Claw, ID  77223     │
│              ◆              │
│      (214) 779-0066         │
│                             │
└─────────────────────────────┘
```

Figure 2-11: Bullets and dingbats can also be used as design elements to separate lines.

How large should bullets be? It's usually best to make them slightly smaller than the capital letters of the typeface used. You want them to look like a checklist, not a giant black pearl necklace. In WP you adjust the size of bullets and dingbats as you would any other text—by selecting them (Alt+F4, then the arrow keys), then selecting "font size" (Ctrl+F8, 2).

Bullets or dingbats are also used to let the reader know that an article has ended. This practice is particularly common in magazines where an article might flow over several pages or jump to the back of the magazine. Many magazines use a tiny logo for this purpose or the initials of the publication title set in a different typeface from the body text.

Figure 2-12: Icons are larger, more detailed dingbats, like the envelope and scissors shown here.

Symbols"—the popular Zapf dingbat set—to see what can be inserted into your documents). Dingbats and icons can also be downloaded as special fonts from CompuServe, electronic bulletin boards, etc. They can also be purchased as character sets or included with drawing programs from third-party vendors. Just as you can purchase a new typeface, you can also purchase sets of bullets, clip art, dingbats and icons. (See the Resource List in the back of this book for vendors.)

RULES, BOXES & BORDERS

Adding lines is yet another way to add visual variety to, as well as organize, your pages. You can put frames around photos or paragraphs. You can divide text into logical units with vertical or horizontal lines ("rules"). Or you can use decorative frames around text, graphics or an entire page. Such lines and frames can also separate elements from the main body of the document and signal the reader that text or graphics within the lines are related.

A *rule* is a straight line. It can be vertical or horizontal, thick or thin, plain or fancy. Rules are used most often to separate the page elements into groups or zones. The most common use of rules is to separate columns. If you choose full justification (which aligns the text on both the left side and the right side of the column), rules are a good idea. With ragged-right alignment (text justified on the left side), rules are often omitted.

Rules are mainly used to separate columns.

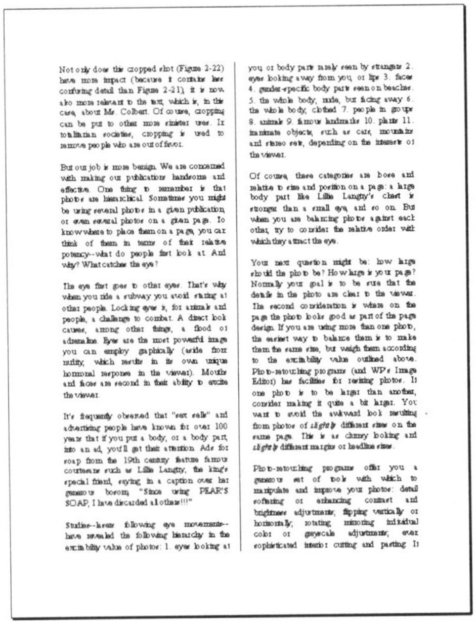

Not only does this cropped shot (Figure 2-22) have more impact (because it contains less confusing detail than Figure 2-21), it is now also more relevant to the text, which is, in this case, about Mr. Colbert. Of course, cropping can be put to other more sinister uses. In totalitarian societies, cropping is used to remove people who are out of favor.

But our job is more benign. We are concerned with making our publications handsome and effective. One thing to remember is that photos are hierarchical. Sometimes you might be using several photos in a given publication, or even several photos on a given page. To know where to place them on a page, you can think of them in terms of their relative potency--what do people first look at. And why? What catches the eye?

The eye first goes to other eyes. That's why when you ride a subway you avoid staring at other people. Locking eyes is, for animals and people, a challenge to combat. A direct look causes, among other things, a flood of adrenaline. Eyes are the most powerful image you can employ graphically (aside from nudity, which results in its own unique hormonal response in the viewer). Mouths and faces are second in their ability to excite the viewer.

It's frequently observed that "sex sells" and advertising people have known for over 100 years that if you put a body, or a body part, into an ad, you'll get their attention. Ads for soap from the 19th century feature famous courtesans such as Lillie Langtry, the king's special friend, saying, in a caption over her generous bosom, "Since using PEAR'S SOAP, I have discarded all others!!!"

Studies--lasers following eye movements--have revealed the following hierarchy in the excitability value of photos: 1. eyes looking at you, or body parts rarely seen by strangers 2. eyes looking away from you, or lips 3. faces 4. gender-specific body parts seen on beaches. 5. the whole body, nude, but facing away 6. the whole body, clothed 7. people in groups 8. animals 9. famous landmarks 10. plants 11. inanimate objects, such as cars, mountains and stereo sets, depending on the interests of the viewer.

Of course, these categories are loose and relative to size and position on a page: a large body part like Lillie Langtry's chest is stronger than a small eye, and so on. But when you are balancing photos against each other, try to consider the relative order with which they attract the eye.

Your next question might be: how large should the photo be? How large is your page? Normally your goal is to be sure that the details in the photo are clear to the viewer. The second consideration is where on the page the photo looks good as part of the page design. If you are using more than one photo, the easiest way to balance them is to make them the same size, but weigh them according to the excitability value outlined above. Photo-retouching programs (and WP's Image Editor) has facilities for resizing photos. If one photo is to be larger than another, consider making it quite a bit larger. You want to avoid the awkward look resulting from photos of *slightly* different sizes on the same page. This is as clumsy looking and *slightly* different margins or headline sizes.

Photo-retouching programs offer you a generous set of tools with which to manipulate and improve your photos: detail softening or enhancing contrast and brightness adjustments, flipping vertically or horizontally, rotating, mirroring individual color or greyscale adjustments, even sophisticated interior cutting and pasting. In

Figure 2-13: If you use full justification for your columns, rules help the reader visually isolate the columns.

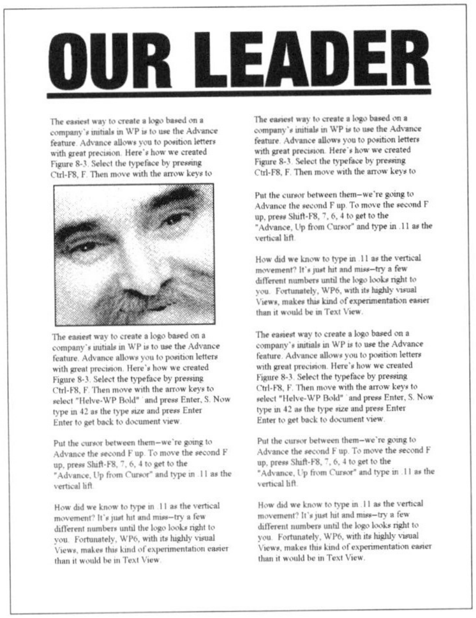

OUR LEADER

The easiest way to create a logo based on a company's initials in WP is to use the Advance feature. Advance allows you to position letters with great precision. Here's how we created Figure 8-3. Select the typeface by pressing Ctrl-F8, F. Then move with the arrow keys to

The easiest way to create a logo based on a company's initials in WP is to use the Advance feature. Advance allows you to position letters with great precision. Here's how we created Figure 8-3. Select the typeface by pressing Ctrl-F8, F. Then move with the arrow keys to select "Helve-WP Bold" and press Enter, S. Now type in 42 as the type size and press Enter Enter to get back to document view.

Put the cursor between them—we're going to Advance the second F up. To move the second F up, press Shift-F8, 7, 6, 4 to get to the "Advance, Up from Cursor" and type in .11 as the vertical lift.

How did we know to type in .11 as the vertical movement? It's just hit and miss—try a few different numbers until the logo looks right to you. Fortunately, WP6, with its highly visual Views, makes this kind of experimentation easier than it would be in Text View.

The easiest way to create a logo based on a company's initials in WP is to use the Advance feature. Advance allows you to position letters with great precision. Here's how we created Figure 8-3. Select the typeface by pressing Ctrl-F8, F. Then move with the arrow keys to

Put the cursor between them—we're going to Advance the second F up. To move the second F up, press Shift-F8, 7, 6, 4 to get to the "Advance, Up from Cursor" and type in .11 as the vertical lift.

How did we know to type in .11 as the vertical movement? It's just hit and miss—try a few different numbers until the logo looks right to you. Fortunately, WP6, with its highly visual Views, makes this kind of experimentation easier than it would be in Text View.

The easiest way to create a logo based on a company's initials in WP is to use the Advance feature. Advance allows you to position letters with great precision. Here's how we created Figure 8-3. Select the typeface by pressing Ctrl-F8, F. Then move with the arrow keys to select "Helve-WP Bold" and press Enter, S. Now type in 42 as the type size and press Enter Enter to get back to document view.

Put the cursor between them—we're going to Advance the second F up. To move the second F up, press Shift-F8, 7, 6, 4 to get to the "Advance, Up from Cursor" and type in .11 as the vertical lift.

How did we know to type in .11 as the vertical movement? It's just hit and miss—try a few different numbers until the logo looks right to you. Fortunately, WP6, with its highly visual Views, makes this kind of experimentation easier than it would be in Text View.

Figure 2-14: You can use a thick rule to emphasize a headline or a title.

single, double, dashed, dotted, thick, extra thick, thin-thick, thick-thin, button top/left line, ...
To work with lines: (Alt+F9, 2, 3). (See Appendix A.)

You can adjust the pattern, color, thickness, spacing, etc., of any of these line styles. You can also create custom lines of your own. All this, of course, can be limited by the capabilities of your printer—it must be able to reproduce the various styles.

A *box* is four rules connected into a rectangle. Boxes are used to frame text or an illustration. WP also provides a set of predefined box styles (Alt+F9, 1, 4). (See Appendix A.)

You don't want to overuse rules and boxes. And fancy frames (large, ornate boxes) are quite out of style. You don't want your page to look like a crowded wall in a frame shop. Instead, use rules and boxes when they're needed, to accomplish a particular design goal. And use frames only rarely—for a good reason.

Use boxes and rules with some discretion.

Use Boxes & Rules to

- ✔ Set off a zone of text, a *sidebar*, that amplifies or adds to information in the main text but is not a necessary part of it.

- ✔ Divide columns (with rules), generally, if text in the columns is not fully justified (aligned left and right).

- ✔ Frame a portion of text with an associated illustration—to show that the illustration belongs with the text.

- ✔ Add a frame to a photograph or figure that doesn't have a defined border.

Figure 2-15: Too many rules and boxes create a fussy, busy, old-fashioned look.

Figure 2-16: Add a frame if an illustration doesn't have a defined border.

borders. Decorative borders are best used only on such designs as formal invitations or pieces where you are deliberately trying to create an old-fashioned look. In other words,
like modern architecture, contemporary page design strives
for a clean, geometric look. This trend has been in effect since
the impact of Picasso and other geometrists (Cubism, etc.).
This bias toward geometric austerity picked up speed during
the no-nonsense war years of the 1940s. And it has been gaining ground ever since—with a brief slip during the psychedelic late 1960s.

Decorative borders, like decorative typefaces, are rarely used these days.

Figure 2-17: Borders and frames are similar to rules, but they can include fancy, decorative shapes, like this border that suggests the Middle East.

GRAPHICS: DIAGRAMS, ILLUSTRATIONS, CLIP ART & PHOTOS

It has been said that a picture is worth a thousand words, but that depends on who is writing the words. It's hard to imagine a picture that could equal what the Bill of Rights has accomplished.

Nonetheless, contemporary page design increasingly uses as much *visual* information as possible. Your finished pages are not merely expected to convey information, they are expected to convey information *attractively*.

Think of your audience when choosing graphics.

You want your pages to look good. And one of the best ways to avoid gray, text-heavy pages is to add illustrations. Of course, besides improving your design, pictures *can* often provide more than a thousand words worth of information. If one of the goals of your publication is to tell the reader what it feels like to visit Seattle, it's much easier if you can include photos of Puget Sound, the monorail, etc. Graphics—human bodies, faces and especially eyes—force people to look. It's a prehistoric reaction: we *have* to look at other people, if only to decide whether we need to protect ourselves or flee.

When selecting any graphic, consider the goals of your publication as well as its audience:

✔ Would the text be enhanced or clarified by graphics?

✔ Is there too much text, with insufficient visual relief?

✔ Are you trying to demonstrate something? (If so, consider step-by-step drawings of the process.)

✔ Is this an advertisement of some kind that will get more attention if graphics are added?

✔ Are you doing a newsletter? Including photos of familiar people or events can greatly add to the appeal of your publication.

Diagrams are combinations of numbers, text and graphics. Most often diagrams are graphs and charts. The purpose of diagrams is to make visual what might not be as easily understood in pure text. For example, a statistic like "Aunt Sally's Pastries is selling 20 percent more pies every year" becomes clearer to readers if they can see how that increase in sales *looks,* as in Figure 2-18:

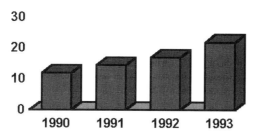

Figure 2-18: Visuals can make statistical information clear.

However, the diagram should be appropriate to the statistics illustrated. A pie chart does a good job of showing percentages (apple pies account for 60 percent of our business) but cannot illustrate changes happening over time (like Aunt Sally's increasing sales) as in Figure 2-19:

Figure 2-19: Wrong: Pie charts are clumsy for displaying data that changes over time.

Though often tedious, sometimes graphs and charts are the best way to explain something to the reader.

ILLUSTRATIONS

Any large graphic that's *drawn* (that's not a diagram or a photo) is an *illustration*. It can be a drawing, an etching, a silhouette—whatever looks good or adds information to your presentation.

CorelDRAW comes with 18,000 pieces of clip art and 750 fonts.

Figure 2-20: Illustrations can powerfully attract the eye. Did you look at anything else on this page first?

CLIP ART

You don't have to be able to draw to include illustrations. There are libraries of "clip art" (collections of predrawn illustrations grouped into various categories such as transportation, food, medicine, animals, etc.) that you can buy. Some programs, such as CorelDRAW or Arts & Letters, come with massive collections of clip art that you can paste into your WordPerfect publications.

gram) and save to disk the clip art illustration you want.
Choose a graphics file format that WP can import. WP has its
own special file format (.WPG for WordPerfect Graphic), and
you can save the file in that format. Then, to bring the clip art
into your WP document, press Alt+G, R, then type in the file
name. Or, another way to import is Alt+F9, 1, 1, 1, then the
file name. WP usually has more than one way to accomplish
something.

   WP itself includes a few .WPG clip art files (see the Resource List for companies that sell clip art collections).

PHOTOS

Photos can be the most powerful graphic element of all. They
are generally full of detail and highly realistic. And they appeal directly to the most robust human sense: vision.

Figure 2-21: People are driven to look at other people. Photos are
hugely attractive (*attractive* in the sense of *magnetic*).

Computers give
us complete
control over
photos—
retouching
has become
relatively easy.

There are many ways you can manipulate photographs to improve design. To help you, there are several excellent photo-retouching programs available. One of these potent computerized tools is CorelPHOTO-PAINT. WP itself provides an "Image Editor," which can accomplish several types of transformation on illustrations and photos (see Chapter 7).

Cropping

When using photographs, your first decision is whether or not to *crop* (trim) the picture—to eliminate unnecessary peripheral details by cutting off one or more edges of the photo. Cropping can make a photo more dramatic, focusing the viewer on the main point. Figure 2-21 is an awkward composition because Cleopatra's hand is cut off. Furthermore, we are doing a story on Claudette Colbert and there is simply no point to including the dying Caesar in this shot. So we crop the photo and Figure 2-22 is the result.

Eliminate
unnecessary and
distracting details
by cropping.

Figure 2-22: Our article is about Ms. Colbert, so we get rid of the rest of the photo by cropping (trimming) it.

Not only does this cropped shot (Figure 2-22) ...

2-21); it is now also more relevant to the text, which in this case, about Ms. Colbert. Of course, cropping can be put to other, more sinister uses. In totalitarian societies, cropping is used to remove people who are out of favor.

Placement on the Page

But our job is more benign. We are concerned with making our publications handsome and effective. Sometimes you might be using several photos in a given publication, or even several photos on a given page. To know where to place them on a page, you can think in terms of a hierarchical order that is defined by the relative potency of each photo: What do people first look at, and why? What catches the eye?

The eye first goes to other *eyes*. That's why when you ride a subway you avoid staring at other people. Locking eyes is, for animals and people, a challenge to combat. A direct look causes, among other things, a flood of adrenaline. Eyes are the most powerful image you can employ graphically (aside from nudity, which results in its own unique hormonal response in the viewer). Mouths and faces are second in their ability to excite the viewer.

It's frequently observed that "sex sells"; and advertising people have known for over 100 years, since advertising first became a science, that putting a body or body part into an ad gets attention. Soap ads from the 19th century featured famous courtesans such as Lillie Langtry, the king's special friend, saying, in a caption over her generous bosom, "Since using PEAR'S SOAP, I have discarded all others!!!"

Be aware of the "magnetism" of various images.

"I have discarded all others!"

Studies—using lasers to follow eye movements—have revealed the following hierarchy in the excitability value of photos:

1. Eyes looking at you, or body parts rarely seen by strangers
2. Eyes looking away from you, or lips
3. Faces
4. Gender-specific body parts seen on beaches
5. The whole body, nude, but facing away
6. The whole body, clothed
7. People in groups
8. Animals
9. Famous landmarks
10. Inanimate objects, such as cars, mountains and stereo sets, depending on the interests of the viewer
11. Plants or vegetables

Of course, these categories are loose and relative to size and position on a page: a large body part like Lillie Langtry's chest is stronger than a small eye, and so on. But when you are balancing photos against each other, try to consider the relative order with which they attract the eye.

Figure 2-23: Eyes, then mouths, are the images most likely to capture a reader's attention.

Figure 2-24: Next in magnetism are faces. After that, body parts, particularly if they are, as here, ambiguous.

Size

Your next question might be: how large should the photo be? How large is your page? Normally your goal is to be sure that the details in the photo are clear to the viewer (and that unnecessary details are removed from the picture).

The second consideration is where on the page the photo looks good as part of the page design. If you are using more than one photo, the easiest way to balance them is to make them the same size, but weigh them according to the excitability value outlined above. Photo-retouching programs (and WP's Image Editor) have facilities for resizing photos. If one photo is to be larger than another, consider making it quite a bit larger. You want to avoid the awkward look resulting from photos of *slightly* different sizes on the same page. This is as clumsy-looking as *slightly* different margins or headline sizes.

Avoid photos or illustrations that are *slightly* different in size.

Altering & Retouching

Photo-retouching programs offer you a generous set of tools with which to manipulate and improve your photos: detail softening or enhancing; contrast and brightness adjustments; flipping vertically or horizontally; rotating; mirroring; individual color or grayscale adjustments; even sophisticated interior cutting and pasting. If you want to remove Trotsky from the collective leadership picture, don't simply *crop* the photo. Instead, clone or cut a tree from the background and paste the tree on top of Trotsky.

When deciding whether and how much to retouch, take a hard look at the photo. Is it too dark? Adjust the brightness and contrast. Is it slightly out of focus? Try edge-detect or sharpness-enhance. There is much you can do within retouching programs to make marginal-quality photos acceptable and good photos splendid.

Boxing

Most photos do not need lines around them: they frame themselves, because they contain enough dark areas to show where the photo ends and the white space of the page begins. You don't want to burden your page with too many rules, frames and boxes. So, don't automatically box your photos.

The primary reason to box a photo is if it contains white areas on one or more sides. In this case, the edge of the photo *will* blend into the white space (momentarily confusing the eye) and a frame is called for to contain it. See Figure 2-16 for an example.

Retouching can make an ordinary photo extraordinary.

Should you frame your photo in a box?

Shadowing

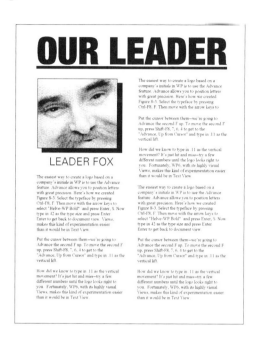

Figure 2-25: Shadowing makes a photo appear to lift and float off the page.

Placing a shadow behind a photo or other illustration can add a three-dimensional look to your page, but this trick should be used sparingly. You need not use a 100 percent black shadow. Often 50 percent or 20 percent black achieves a more subtle effect, since 100 percent shadows in the real world are found only in dungeons and at midnight in the wilderness.

In WP, shadows can be added to Graphics Boxes easily. There's a special "Shadow" menu where you can specify position, size and color for any shadow. Press Alt+F9, 1, 1, 2 (to add the picture to the Graphics Box). Select 1 "Image on Disk" then 1 (Filename) to import the image into the box. Then select 6 (Edit Border/Fill), 5, 1, 5 (select "lower-right" for your shadow position—this is by far the most attractive

WordPerfect makes shadowing easy.

and most familiar shadow position). Then press Enter to get out of the menus. If you are in Graphics View, save the file (F10) and you should see your image redrawn onscreen.

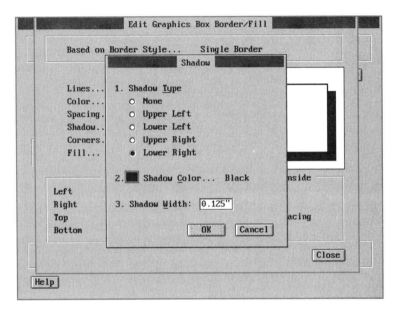

Figure 2-26: Define and add a shadow to a Graphics Box in this Shadow window.

Silhouetting

When you remove all or most of the background from a photo, you give yourself an interesting visual object to place into your page. It can serve the same purpose as an icon in some cases, symbolizing a section of a publication (a football could symbolize the sports section of a newsletter). WP doesn't have facilities for silhouetting, but most drawing or retouching programs do (see the Resource List).

Having an image burst out of its frame can be a powerful attractor.

Figure 2-27: Silhouetting means "cutting" an image out from its background. The sculpture on the right is more dramatic against the white background.

A similar technique involves removing a portion of the photo from one or more sides, except for a particular detail. The detail then is exposed and seems to thrust out of the page toward the viewer.

Figure 2-28: This partial silhouetting pulls the plane right out of the picture, and pulls the reader's eye into your page.

Figure 2-29: The subject's eyes will attract the viewer, not to mention its horns.

But for a stronger image, remove some background and give the beast *dimension*.

Figure 2-30: With silhouetting, the creature now seems to be poking *through* your page.

Silhouetting used to ...
.... and lots of patience. (It's where we get the
term *clip art*.) And the results would look coarse unless you
were most careful. However, computer photo-retouching
programs such as CorelPHOTO-PAINT and Adobe's Photoshop make this task (and others, like removing unwanted
objects *inside* a photo) much easier.

Silhouetting is
easy these days:
no more scissors.

Digitizing Photographs

Just as with clip art, you can download photographs from
CompuServe, America Online and bulletin boards. A photo
will be in a .GIF, .PCX, .TIF or other graphics file format and
can be retrieved into WP just like clip art and other images.
To digitize your own photos from books, magazines or your
personal collection, you can purchase an inexpensive hand-
held scanner. A *hand-scanner* is a small plastic gadget about
the size of your fist that plugs into your computer. You drag
the scanner across the page of a magazine and the picture is
translated into the digital format that the computer can store
in a file, display on a monitor and print.

Where do you
get photos?

　　To get the best, most realistic-looking scans, you should try
to purchase a *256-level* grayscale scanner. This will give you
256 gradations of gray and will look quite sharp and good
onscreen or on the printed page. (See the Resource List for
recommendations.)

Violate Zone Limits

A primary modern design rule: It's often a good idea to violate expected space. Here are some ways to violate space:
Pictures are usually square, so make one part of the picture
jut out from the squareness. (In other words, silhouette it.)
Objects are usually separated, so overlap some of them.
Things are usually enclosed within a frame or a page, so
make some of the things stick out beyond their frame or
page. All of these moves make your work more *dimensional*,
more *free,* and often considerably more visually exciting. If
you are creating an ad for an airline, maybe you could pull
the end of a line of text *up* a little, like a take-off.

Modern design breaks out of frames often.

Use space violation with caution.

Take a look at a well-designed ad or a stylish magazine (such as *Interview*, the *New Yorker*, *Spy* or *Vanity Fair*). Notice how often things go off the page, cover each other up or shove off beyond their frame. In fact, how many ads can you find in these magazines where everything stays *within* its frame or page?

What you are doing when you trespass zone expectations is to make viewers come to grips with what they see. They have to translate your images a little, they must interpret the things they are seeing (just as they do in real life). Escaping images will seem to be getting loose, perhaps dangerously leaping toward the reader.

Done with restraint, violations like this can make a composition seem more *real*. The world is not flat and packaged into neat zones. When you enter a restaurant, someone is standing in front of someone else. Someone else is partly in your peripheral vision and partly beyond it—going off the "page." In the real world, things are not packaged into frames and pages.

When you employ these techniques, you are forcing your viewers to reconcile their expectations (paper is flat and has borders) with what they are, in fact, seeing on your page—something is on top of something else or something is going off or coming out of this page. Of course you don't want to overdo this or your work will look messy and disorganized, or, worse, hectic and chaotic. A space violation once every few pages (or one or two within a given ad) is enough to open things up and refresh or stimulate the viewer.

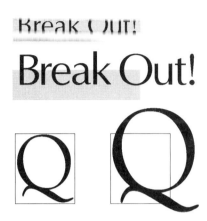

Figure 2-31: Violations of expected space will make your graphics more dimensional, vivid and real.

MOVING ON

We've discussed the large obvious objects—blocks of text, photos and so on. In the next chapter we'll turn our attention to the smaller and more subtle issues. The typefaces you choose, the distance between individual letters in a headline (kerning), the distance between the lines and paragraphs in the body text (leading), and other seemingly minor issues all contribute to the appearance and ultimate success of your publication.

Most readers are not conscious of these less-dramatic elements of your design. But the design, for example, of the typeface you've selected can make your work look either crude and amateurish or polished and professional. These "lesser" elements are like spices in cooking—they aren't the primary substance, but they contribute quite a bit to the quality of the final product.

You should try to be conscious of things the reader *senses* but doesn't think.

3 Refining the Text

In this chapter we'll explore your options when choosing typefaces, type sizes, type weights, letter spacing and word spacing. It might seem surprising, but these seemingly minor decisions will have a major impact on the appearance of your publication.

Readers are more aware of the content of what they're reading than they are of the design of the letters in the text. In fact, most people don't pay attention to the hundreds of different designs for the letters of the alphabet.

However, to the typographer, desktop publisher or graphic artist, selecting a typeface is a serious issue. For one thing, a poor selection can make text less readable. For another thing, readers can be made either comfortable or uneasy depending on how well the type suits the purpose, tone and message of the text.

Because your choice of typeface will have a significant impact on your reader, we are going to devote several pages to typefaces, the subtleties of their designs and their suitability for various purposes.

Selecting a typeface is more important than you might think.

TYPES OF TYPE

The most basic guideline when choosing typefaces is to use *sans-serif* type for headlines and *serif* type for body text. Many contemporary publications, ads and other professionally produced documents follow this custom.

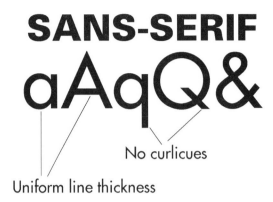

Sans-serif type has a stripped-down, sleek and contemporary look.

No curlicues

Uniform line thickness

Figure 3-1: Sans-serif characters, like those in WordPerfect's Univers typeface, are, with only a few exceptions, without finishing strokes, or curlicues, and have almost no variation in line (stroke) thickness.

Curlicues

Variations in thickness

Figure 3-2: Serifs are additional strokes that imitate the thinning line caused by lifting a pen from paper. See WP's Times, Roman (except Swiss Roman), and Dutch typefaces.

Serif typeface designs offer many variations of line thickness and added strokes, bubbles, and tails at the ends of the letters. These features help the reader differentiate the characters from each other, which is the main reason that serif is often easier to read than sans, particularly for small text, and why serif is almost always the choice for body text.

Sans typefaces are bolder, simpler, stronger-looking. (Some sans faces *do* have slight, almost imperceptible, variations in stroke thickness—see the lowercase *a* in Figure 3-1.) But as a rule, sans is used for large text (headlines, subheads,

... .

often set in boldface. Its main purpose is to attract the reader to the story or article.)

Figure 3-3: You can use sans to set off a "pull-quote" from the body text.

MUTANT, IN-BETWEEN TYPEFACES

There are a few typefaces that combine the best qualities of serif and sans styles (note "Optima" in Figure 3-5). They feature relatively subdued yet noticeable line width variation and tiny, nearly invisible, serifs here and there. Such lettering is more often used in headlines than in body text, but it can, with care, be used for both purposes (particularly if there isn't too much body text). We'll have more to say about Optima later. It's one of the loveliest faces around.

THE EVOLUTION OF TYPEFACE DESIGN

All serif typefaces derive from a classic, elegant alphabet designed by an obscure Roman calligrapher in the first century A.D. This seminal typeface consisted entirely of capital letters and was so thoughtfully designed and close to perfection that it continues to dominate Western printed text and probably always will. The Roman typeface was originally used for inscriptions chiseled into marble—on temples and statues—but it proved equally suited to ink on paper.

The second major change in typeface design took place in 1816. Famous alphabet designer William Caslon anticipated the simplified, spare designs which were to later dominate the artistic styles of the 20th century: he lopped off all the extra strokes, curlicues and flourishes (the serifs) and created the first *sans*-serif alphabet. (To be precise, the Greek alphabet of 500 B.C. was without serifs; but Roman has been so dominant that sans-serif disappeared for 2,000 years until Caslon chopped off the flourishes.)

Sans-serif typefaces are now used for most headlines, captions, pull-quotes or any text positioned apart from, or larger than, the body text. The most popular sans-serif typefaces are called *Helvetica* or *Swiss* (see WP's Helve, Swiss and Univers).

All roads lead to Rome.

AaBb&Qq	Avant Garde
AaBb&Qq	**Futura Bold**
AaBb&Qq	Futura Condensed
AABB&QQ	**MACHINE**
AaBb&Qq	Optima
AaBb&Qq	Helvetica
AaBb&Qq	Helvetica Light
AaBb&Qq	Helvetica Narrow
AaBb&Qq	**Helvetica Black**

Figure 3-4: Examples of the sans-serif style.

Most typefaces have several "flavors," or appearance variations, including boldface, italic and underlining. Boldface is most often used in headlines. Boldface is big, black and thick. Only rarely do you see it within body text, because it tends to be more a distraction than a help to the reader. People sometimes mistakenly assume that using boldface is a good way to add emphasis to certain words in the body text.

Other bad ways to emphasize text are all-capital letters, reversed type (white-on-black), underlined words and numerous exclamation points. These crutches should not be used as substitutes for adding emphasis via the writing, the choice of words.

In body text, you should generally avoid boldface, reverses and underlining; and limit the use of exclamation points to an actual exclamation within quotation marks (as in "We *must* win!" the chairman said). The reason you want to remove the faux emphasis is that it can make writing look hysterical, childish or both. What's more, it's self-defeating since you cannot emphasize several dozen words per page and expect that the emphasis will retain its original strength. Instead of modulating the voice, the speaker ends up merely shouting.

There are, however, a few instances where using boldface selectively in body text can be beneficial. In particular, a late-breaking news column or rumor column in a newsletter article can benefit from boldface used to highlight company or individual names. This is an effective way of letting the reader skim through the text, looking for names or topics of interest. It's rather like using embedded subheads as a way of outlining and highlighting the various subjects in the article.

Boldface is rarely used in body text.

Underlined text, too, is rare in modern publications. When people wrote letters on typewriters, underlining was used to signify *italics* (yet another way—and the best way—to add emphasis to a word). Only the most advanced typewriters (such as the IBM Selectric, designed just before typewriters became obsolete) offered an italic typeface option. So underlining was used instead. Underlining is happily passing into history.

The italic version of a typeface is, however, an exception to the rule. It is unobtrusive, quite attractive and valuable. Italics do look somewhat like script—slanted to the right, thinner, more rounded, with a connected quality, as if a writer were not lifting the pen from the paper between strokes. (When you want to emphasize something *within* an italic passage, revert to normal, nonitalicized letters to achieve the same effect.)

> Underlining is almost never used in typeset text.

CHOOSING TYPEFACES

If you can manage it, acquire additional typefaces beyond the ones which come with WP. You'll have an easier time creating the appropriate look and feel for your documents if you have more than the four basic fonts—Sans, Serif, Decorative (Bodoni) and fake handwriting (Commercial Script)—supplied with WP.

attached to your printer, or downloadable typefaces on disk
(in addition to TT's rather limited selection), what typefaces
should you use? It depends on your goals, but here are some
general guidelines.

What typefaces should you use?

Garamond is perhaps the oldest typeface that is still extremely popular. Garamond will probably be around as long
as people use Western alphabets. It's an excellent all-around
choice for body text. Another good face for body text is
Palatino. The somewhat less antique-looking Times (Roman
or Dutch) faces are also safe choices for body text.

Special Note: You might be puzzled if you buy a set of
typefaces and discover names such as *Gourmand* instead of
Garamond, or *Palomino* for *Palatino*. The reason for this is, we
have reached such a state of legal smothering that individual
words can be copyrighted. Some companies which design
typefaces have registered the names of the classic faces.

So, given that a typeface is sometimes called something
other than its real name, how do you know what typeface
you're dealing with? Look at the uppercase Q and amper-
sand (&). Those two characters usually are quite distinctive
in each face, so if your characters match theirs, you've got it.

The Goudy and Caslon typefaces—though they're both
quite attractive—have fallen into disfavor these days because
to some eyes they look a little fussy and out-of-date. More's
the pity, perhaps.

Goudy and Caslon are out of favor today.

AaBb&Qq	Garamond
AaBb&Qq	Palatino
AaBb&Qq	Times Roman
AaBb&Qq	Goudy Hundred
AaBb&Qq	Goudy Old-Style
AaBb&Qq	Caslon
AaBb&Qq	USA Light
AaBb&Qq	**USA Black**
AaBb&Qq	Optima

Figure 3-5: Excellent alternative typefaces you might want to add to those that WP supplies.

Univers, a sans-serif face, was created by Adrian Frutiger in this century. It looks good in headlines, captions and even body text (when there isn't a lot of body text on the page).

Univers is highly geometrical. Considerable symmetry results from each letter having the same line widths, no matter in which direction the line is heading.

The uniformity of Univers's characters has a special benefit for desktop publishers. The shapes can be described in relatively simple mathematics, so the computer can print Univers more quickly than it can print other fonts. For the same reasons, Univers fonts often come in a very wide variety of weights and styles (light, bold, heavy, condensed, expanded, etc.). Univers can be easily transformed by the computer into various flavors. Best of all, Univers is very readable. But if you want a really *fat* face, you'll have to buy one—WP doesn't supply a truly thick typeface.

deserves special mention, in my opinion. It is a modern face, created to bridge the gap between sans-serif and serif. The designer, Herman Zapf, wanted the letters of this typeface to be easily readable, like serif fonts. But he also wanted the clean, modern look and the flexibility of a sans face; so he created a design virtually without serifs but gave the necessary definition to the letter shapes through variations in line thickness. He succeeded in combining the virtues of serif and sans-serif type (then he named his face after the word *optimal*).

Like Univers for headlines, and Garamond or Times Roman for body text, you cannot go far wrong if you select Optima. And Optima often looks good in headlines as well. Optima is easy on the eye, flows smoothly across the page and—though modern—is one of the nicest sets of letters ever drawn. Of course, if you're doing a document such as a fax form or a prospectus, use Times or Garamond for body text—or even Palatino—not Optima. Optima might be an effective, attractive face, but it will not convey that touch of formality (or stiffness) that official documents usually require. For formal headlines, use a traditional sans face like Univers.

ORNATE TYPEFACES

During the dark ages, swarms of monks were spending their lives copying devotional texts, prayer books and the Bible. These monks wouldn't leave well enough alone: they drew pictures and even elaborate decorative letterforms in the margins. You could still see the basic shape of the letter, but it was filled and surrounded by grapes, stars, angels in flight or whatever seemed good at the time.

Over the years, whole new alphabets were designed, featuring acrobats twisted into letter shapes, letterforms made out of flowers, and all the rest. If it bends, somebody sometime has used it to design letters. Nowadays, though, these arty typefaces are very, very rarely used.

especially attractive face.

Choose a typeface based on the nature of the publication and the image you want to project.

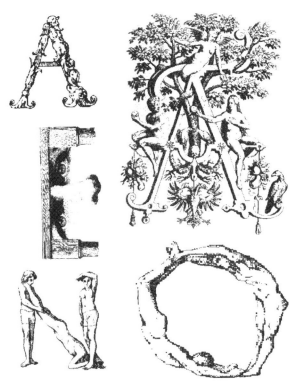

Figure 3-6: Decorative typefaces have been out of fashion since the end of the art deco period in the 1930s.

SELECTING TYPE SIZES

Most computers and printers today feature *scalable* typefaces. This means that you can print at virtually any size—from tiny "mouse type" (4 or 6 points, used for Registered Trademark legalese) to huge headlines (72 points, for example). What are *points*? A point is a unit of measurement that typographers, typesetters and the printing trade use to specify the size of type characters. Most books and other publications use 9-point, 10-point or 11-point characters for body text, and sizes ranging from 20-point to 40-point for headlines.

Scalable typefaces can be printed at almost any size.

what less technical way: fine, small, large, very large, extra large. These are percentages of the "Normal" size, respectively: 60, 80, 120, 150 and 200 percent.

Two things to remember about type size. First, you'll want to limit yourself to three or four type sizes per publication. Too many different sizes will confuse the reader and make your pages look cluttered and disorganized. The same problem occurs when you use too many typefaces. In both cases, the reader ends up having less confidence in the professionalism and message of your publication. It's rather like the effect you'd have on people if you wore several unrelated garments. One way to add variety, without changing typeface or type size, is to select different type *weights* (called Black, Heavy, Expanded, Condensed, etc.). We'll discuss weights in detail later in this chapter.

The second point to consider is that the typeface should be appropriate to the space allotted to it on the page. If you use a small typeface within a large white area, the effect is oddly disconcerting. And equally unattractive is large type within a small amount of white space. It looks squeezed and uncomfortable, like a heavyset person wearing shorts.

D on't make your pages look like a kidnapper's ransom note.

WORDPERFECT TYPEFACES

The typefaces WP makes available to you out of the box depend on the capabilities of your printer. However, most printers can handle WP's basic set of fonts. WP 6.0 comes with seven basic typefaces: Bodoni Bold, Commercial Script, Courier, Dutch (Roman), Helve-WP, Roman-WP and Swiss. Like most computer typefaces today, most of these are *scalable*—they can be printed at any size. (If you see *cpi*—characters-per-inch—following the typeface's name, it's not scalable.) WP calls scalable fonts *graphics fonts,* meaning that to use them your printer must be capable of printing graphics.

WP comes with a set of serviceable, if limited, typefaces.

Find out which typefaces are built into your printer.

Also, as a general rule, graphics fonts will print out more slowly. Remember to change WP's default setting (Medium Graphics print quality) to High Graphics by pressing Shift+F7, G, H.

In addition to these fonts, your printer will have at least one, probably more, built-in fonts. For example, attach a Hewlett-Packard LaserJet III to your computer and its built-in fonts are listed along with WP's fonts when you press Ctrl+F8 to access the font menu. The LaserJet comes with CG Times, Courier, Line Printer and Univers.

Bodoni-WP Bold (Type 1)
CG Times   **CG Times Bold**   *CG Times Bold Italic*   *CG Times Italic*
CommercialScript-WP (Type 1)

Courier 10 Bold (Speedo)	***Courier 10 Bold Italic***
Courier 10 Italic (Speedo)	Courier 10 Roman (Speedo)
Courier 10cpi	**Courier 10cpi Bold**
Courier 10cpi Italic	Courier 12cpi
Courier 12cpi Bold	*Courier 12cpi Italic*
Courier-WP (Type 1)	**Courier-WP Bold (Type 1)**
Dutch 801 Bold (Speedo)	***Dutch 801 Bold Italic (Speedo)***
Dutch 801 Italic (Speedo)	Dutch 801 Roman (Speedo)
Helve-WP (Type 1)	**Helve-WP Bold (Type 1)**
Line Printer 16.67cpi	
Roman-WP (Type 1)	**Roman-WP Bold (Type 1)**
Roman-WP Bold Italic (Type 1)	
Swiss 721 Bold (Speedo)	Swiss 721 Roman (Speedo)
Univers **Univers Bold**	***Univers Bold Italic* *Univers Italic***

Figure 3-7: Several typefaces are built into a LaserJet III printer; the rest come with WP.

If you don't use a LaserJet or compatible, you'll probably notice some minor differences between the fonts available to you and those listed in Figure 3-7. Usually you'll get some extra faces which are built into your printer. For instance, the Okidata ML192 printer doesn't have CG Times, Line Printer or Univers. But it does have 11 different sizes and styles of "Prestige," an old typewriter monospaced font like Courier. However, all the other fonts shown in Figure 3-7 are available to the Okidata.

a macro which will bring up all the typefaces (switch to
Graphics View, Ctrl+F3, then press Alt+F10, then type in
"Allfonts" as the macro name). Even if your screen cannot
display the fonts, you can still print them on your printer for
future reference.

Let's take a brief tour of the typefaces shown in Figure 3-7
and discuss the uses for each:

✔ **Courier** is probably the most well-known of the typewriter typefaces. Courier is rarely used these days because it, like other typewriter faces, does not adjust the
spacing: each letter takes up as much room as every
other letter. It's much easier to read text with *proportional* letter spacing—where the *i* takes up less room
than the *m*.

Computerized typesetting can produce beautiful,
proportionally spaced type, which makes your final
product look much more professional.

Why avoid Courier and other *monospaced* fonts like
Prestige for body text? Studies have shown that proportional fonts (most computer typefaces are proportional)
can be read 30 percent faster and use about 35 percent
less paper because each character only takes up as
much room as necessary.

✔ **Roman-WP** is one of three faces in this list which are
based on the classic Roman design. This (or Dutch
Roman) is your best choice for body text in almost any
document. The differences between these Roman typefaces are subtle, but notice that some are heavier
(thicker, closer to boldface) than others. Also, the serifs
differ in subtle ways—compare the capital *C* or *Q*.

✔ **Bodoni Bold-WP** is the only decorative, nontraditional
font supplied with WP. It is a serif font, like Roman, but
it's reminiscent of the 1930s in its tuxedo-like black-
and-white contrasts. This penguin effect is achieved by
making some parts of letters extremely thick and dark,

Courier is hard
to read and looks
amateurish.

Bodoni-WP is
WP's only
decorative font.

attached to other lines which are razor-thin (see the *W*). The rule of thumb about decorative fonts is, don't use them unless they are in harmony with the topic of your publication. It's too bold for much body text, but Bodoni would work in headlines in advertisements for retro-theme dances or war surplus sales.

✔ **CG Times** comes with the LaserJet printer and is that printer's variation on the classic body text Roman font. It is serviceable but a little heavy. The lines are thicker than Roman-WP (though less thick than Dutch 801 Roman). Compare the lowercase *o*. These things are a matter of preference, but of these two rival Romans, my choice would be WP's "Roman-WP" because the lighter your body text, the less gray (less threatening) the masses of text appear to the reader. And, it follows, the more likely it is that readers will actually read what you are publishing. Of course, if there isn't much text on your page, you might well opt for a darker look to balance the headlines or graphics.

✔ **Commercial Script** is used mainly for wedding invitations and certain kinds of restaurant menus. Script unashamedly tries to look like deluxe handwriting. For several centuries, ending in Edwardian times, it was possible to hire somebody to hand-letter your calling cards and the invitations to your parties and balls. Hand-lettering can be quite elegant. Mechanically imitated, the results are, at best, faux elegant. Besides, who has handwriting like that these days, with all those flourishes and tight curls? Script type has joined the lace hanky in that museum of things that are too much trouble and too ornate for our contemporary lifestyle.

✔ **Dutch 801 Roman** sounds like a good name for a locomotive. It is the thickest, and the bolder, of WP's two flavors of the classic body text face. It's handsomely designed and would be good where your page has sufficient white space (where sections of body text are brief or widely spaced). It's a formal-looking Roman

CG Times is a slightly bold classic Roman face.

WP's "fancy" Commercial Script has very limited uses.

Dutch 801 Roman is a serviceable sans-serif face.

wall charts, stationery, instruction manuals, some catalogs, company reports and prospectuses. Use it when
you *want* your piece to look serious.

✔ **Helve-WP** competes with WP's other sans-serif font,
Swiss 721 (confusingly named Swiss Roman—this is
not a Roman font). The winner of this competition is for
you to decide; which of these two headline/pull-
quote/teaser/caption (anything that's not body text)
typefaces should you use? Helve is a slight bit heavier
and darker, a little thicker (compare the capital *R*), but
not all that much different.

✔ **Line Printer** is like Courier, a holdover from an earlier
technology. It's built into the LaserJet printer, is quite
tiny, and imitates the output of early computer printers.
Not of much use for anything in desktop publishing.

✔ **Roman WP** is my favorite of WP's body text typefaces.
It's lighter and more airy than Dutch Roman. Use it
when you want your pages to look less formidable, less
gray. It's particularly good when you've got a lot of text
on a page and relatively little white space.

Roman WP is a good choice for most body text.

✔ **Swiss Roman** is confusingly named since Swiss or
Helve typefaces are sans-serif and Roman or Dutch are
serif. (Swiss Roman is also known as Swiss 721.) In any
case, the differences between this font and Helve-WP
are slight. It's another sans face.

✔ **Univers** is the LaserJet printer's built-in sans-serif face.
Because Univers is *just a little like serif faces*, you might
want to use it instead of the two sans faces included
with WP. It varies the line widths just a little in the lowercase letters (the WP sans lines are all the same). This
variation in width simply looks better on the page than
rigidly uniform stroke widths. And it's easier to read.
To see the difference, compare *b, m, n* and *t*.

Univers's varia-
tions in line
thickness give it a
slightly serif
quality.

SELECTING TYPE WEIGHTS

You normally don't want to use more than two or three typefaces in a given publication. More than four and you start to get that kidnapper's ransom note effect. However, you can add variety without creating a cluttered, confused look by selecting different type *weights*. Some fonts come in several weights, meaning variations in the width of the strokes and the width of the letters. These alternatives are similar to the difference between Helve and Helve Bold. However, they go beyond this to offer thin, very thick and other options. There are various names for these optional weights: *condensed, expanded, black, heavy, light*, etc. You'll see alternative type weights listed together in "type families."

The typefaces that come with WP do not contain alternative weights, but you can purchase printer cartridges, printer "wheels" or downloadable soft fonts which do often include several weights. However, the trend today—with such programs as CorelPHOTO-PAINT, Windows and other graphics applications—is to supply many dozens of typefaces and various weights for some of the more popular faces. Downloadable typefaces are also available free on bulletin boards, CompuServe, America Online and so on. Figure 3-8 lists some of the alternative type weights available in CorelPHOTO-PAINT for the Switzerland (Helve) typeface.

Type weight is the thickness of the letters.

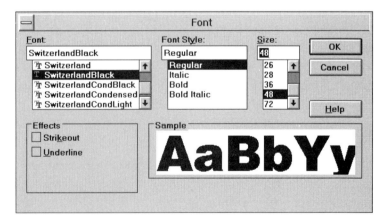

Figure 3-8: Various type weights, if offered, will be listed together, with such names as *condensed, light* and *black,* in WP's font-selection window.

There are, of course, th   l   l l li

tridges to your printer, get them free from BBS— (b all i
board systems), or buy programs such as CorelDRAW that
come with hundreds of fonts.

Figure 3-9: A scattering of design interpretations and type weights
of the letter *a*.

SELECTING & CHANGING FONTS

WP provides you with three ways to change fonts. If you
want to change the default font which will be used whenever
you start a new document, press Shift+F8, 4, 3.

Or there are two ways to change fonts within a document.
First, position your cursor at the start of the text where you
want the font to change, and "select" the text with Alt+F4,
then move with the arrow keys to highlight the text you want
to change. A second way: if you have the Ribbon visible (see
the View menu), you can just select a new font from it. If not,

Changing fonts
within a
document is
easy.

then press Ctrl+F8, 1, and you'll see your choice of fonts. After you select a font (and optionally change its size or other attributes), WP will insert a code into the document to specify the change(s) you've made. You can always look at these codes and even delete them by typing Alt+F3.

DOWNLOADING FONTS

If you have purchased or acquired downloadable ("soft") fonts from a bulletin board or another program, you can have WP send them to your printer. (This assumes that you have a printer which can accept them. Some printers don't have enough built-in memory.) First you need to tell WP where you have stored your soft fonts (in which directory):

Shift+F7, S, E then 7. Enter the directory where your soft fonts are stored, then go back to the normal WP screen and specify which downloadable fonts to send to the printer's memory: Ctrl+F8, Shift+F1, 3. Select Soft Fonts, Edit, Edit to see a list of soft fonts.

Some of the fonts in this list will be ones that WP *assumes* you have, based on the printer you have—they are fonts sold by the printer manufacturer. Others on the list will be any you have on your disk in the directory you specified under printer setup (Shift+F7, S, E).

At this point you will notice several things. Some fonts will have numbers after them such as 12 cpi . This means the font size is 12 characters per inch. Others will be measured in *points*, such as 10pt. Note that these are not *scalable* fonts— you cannot specify just any type size—you must pick a size from the list of what's there.

In addition, some fonts may be marked Land (for *landscape*). Some printers can print two ways: the normal way for most documents is called *portrait* orientation (because it's the shape of most painted portraits). Landscape (you can guess how it gets its name) is shaped more like a movie screen: the page is wider than it is long.

(In WP, you can switch to landscape orientation with Shift+F8, 3, 4. The usual default setting is Letter (portrait) which is the standard 8½- x 11-inch paper, with the page

Soft fonts can add variety to your work.

Landscape orientation means printing sideways—the long way—on a page.

oriented vertically. But

printed sideways on the page.

Also, you can mark the fonts for automatic downloading when you first start WP. This option is good if your printer has enough memory to hold all your favorite fonts and if you use these fonts frequently enough to have them immediately available while you're working. Such fonts are marked with an asterisk (*).

The alternative is to mark a font with a plus sign (+), which tells WP to download the font if you request it. This option is best for fonts you use infrequently. The downloading will slow things up during a print job as soft fonts are loaded into the printer, but you can repeatedly change the font or font size this way without worrying that you might run out of printer memory to hold all the different typefaces.

If you have just selected some fonts to be automatically downloaded each time WP starts but don't want to restart WP, you can force those fonts to be downloaded: Shift+F7, 8.

FONT CARTRIDGES

Cartridges are the easiest way to add more typefaces to your repertoire—you just plug the cartridge into your printer the same way you plug in a new Nintendo game. These fonts don't have to be sent to the printer's memory each time the printer is turned on, as do downloadable fonts. They become part of the printer's capabilities. Most of these fonts are not scalable, but several type sizes will be included. There are a number of popular cartridges, some containing large numbers of fonts. But remember that not all typefaces are of equal quality (some can look rough, or too dark, or simply be crudely designed).

Caveat Emptor: It's best not to rely on the samples printed in magazines or on the cartridge's box. Magazines and ads are printed at much higher resolutions than home computer printers can achieve. Instead, ask to see a real-world printout using the same printer you will use. Then ask yourself, are the lowercase letters finely drawn with no rough edges or breaks in the thin lines? Are the font weights that are in-

Cartridges are the simplest and most efficient way to add typefaces.

cluded ones you use regularly? Is there enough variety in the selection? Perhaps the best cartridge for general use with the LaserJet is the "F" cartridge, "Tms Proportional 2." It's a good, serviceable classic Roman face. But WP's Roman faces are quite good, and so many excellent downloadable fonts these days are practically free—you might want to explore that source before buying a cartridge.

To let WP know that you are using a cartridge, use Ctrl+F8, Shift+F1, Cartridge, Edit.

CONTROL OVER SPACING

It's risky, but you can add an avant-garde look to your publication by using a sans-serif typeface for body text. However, because of its lack of character differentiation, you should set the lines of a sans face fairly far apart (add "leading").

Leading

In WP, you adjust the leading by pressing Shift+F8, 1, 3. Then select the distance between the lines. To get the amount of leading illustrated in Figure 3-10, use 1.2.

Add lead in body text, but reduce lead in headlines.

Body text can be in sans-serif, but you want to provide lots of white space by separating the lines more than you would when using serif typefaces. It can look smooth and contemporary, but would be tiresome to read in large quantities. Body sans is rarely used because readers are accustomed to, and more comfortable, reading serif body text.

Figure 3-10: Put extra space between lines if you use sans-serif for body text.

you pull them closer together by *reducing* the default leading. If you don't remove some of that white space, readers may think that each line in the headline is a separate topic.

Figure 3-11: Reduce white space between the lines of headlines and subheads, to tighten and unify the message.

Paragraph Spacing

In addition to the distance between lines of text, you can also adjust the space between paragraphs. Using some extra white space here can open up your document and make it appear less formidable to the reader. Sure, it's psychological and illusory (there's still just as much text to read), but many contemporary readers prefer their text in bite-size pieces.

To change paragraph spacing, Shift+F8, 2, 8. Then, adjust paragraph spacing from the default 1 to 1.7 to create the look in Figure 3-12.

Figure 3-12: Thanks to MTV, *USA Today* and other influences, readers increasingly like paragraphs that are separated by some extra white space. It makes the text look less demanding.

KERNING

Most typefaces (except Courier and a few other *monospaced* typefaces) have variations in the spaces between the letters. *Kerning* allows you to make additional adjustments to letter spacing—specifically to bring certain letters closer together. Kerning is almost exclusively applied to headlines, where the large type sizes make too much space between some pairs of letters highly visible.

Why kern headlines? Because your work will look more professional and be more readable. Studies have shown that people don't read text one letter at a time. Instead, most readers glance at each word and, almost instantly, recognize the *shape* of the entire word. If you tighten some of its interior spaces, you graphically emphasize that word's unique shape.

You don't need to kern everything, but if some characters in a headline look too loosely spaced to you, a little manual adjustment is called for. Kerning is often needed when an

Usually, kerning is needed for headlines only.

instructions within your text to make it bold, italicize it, change spacing, etc. Move the cursor around in the code view and you'll see some of the abbreviations (such as [Wrd/Ltr Spacing]) expand to reveal the precise settings. Notice in Figure 3-14 that our two sections of kerned letters are embraced by [Wrd/Ltr Spacing] codes.

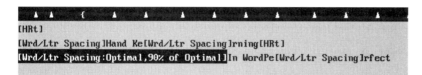

Figure 3-14: WP's code view shows you which letters have been kerned.

Even Finer Kerning Control

WP usually offers more than one way to get a job done. The Advance feature works quite well when you want to kern. We described letter spacing adjustments above, but for the finest possible control, you can adjust each letter pair with Advance. Advance positions the cursor in highly precise ways (you can advance up, down, right or left of the current position, but for kerning, we'll want to advance left to tighten the letters).

Kern individual letters with Advance.

Our Kern/Kernoff pair allowed us to kern groups of letters (just the way italicizing affects groups of letters). But when using Advance, the effect will only be between a single pair of letters—the letters located on either side of the current cursor position.

Using Advance sounds tedious, but, again, if you record this as a macro, it's virtually instant. Here's how. Put your cursor between the letter pair you want to kern. Press Shift+F8, 7, 6, 1, and type in .01. This will move the character on the right of the cursor $1/100$th of an inch to the left, removing a little space. Do this as many times as you want until you get precisely the spacing you like.

You can go the other way, too, increasing the space between individual letters to create a special effect. Used with all-capital letters, this trick is a nice way of adding a title to a regularly published column or drawing attention to a particular article. You follow the same procedure as you do to kern, except you select, usually, much more than 100 percent of Optimal. In Figure 3-15 we used 400 percent.

Separated letters can look clean and formal in special headlines.

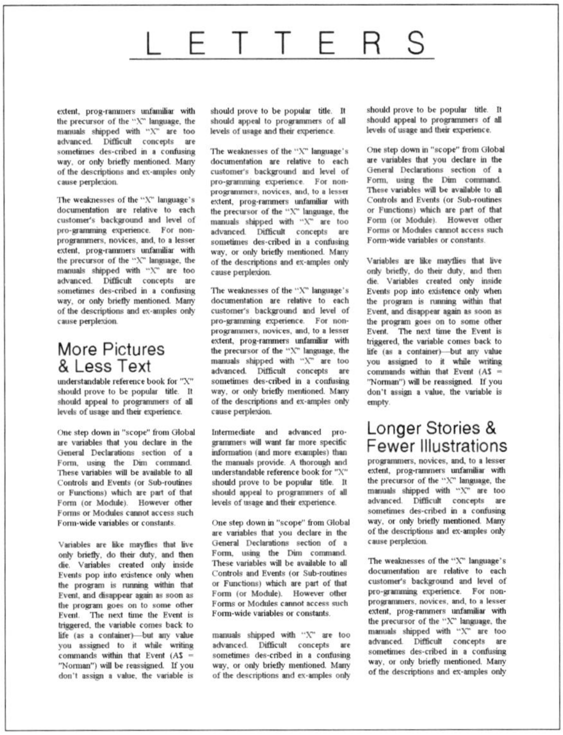

L E T T E R S

extent, prog-rammers unfamiliar with the precursor of the "X" language, the manuals shipped with "X" are too advanced. Difficult concepts are sometimes des-cribed in a confusing way, or only briefly mentioned. Many of the descriptions and ex-amples only cause perplexion.

The weaknesses of the "X" language's documentation are relative to each customer's background and level of pro-gramming experience. For non-programmers, novices, and, to a lesser extent, prog-rammers unfamiliar with the precursor of the "X" language, the manuals shipped with "X" are too advanced. Difficult concepts are sometimes des-cribed in a confusing way, or only briefly mentioned. Many of the descriptions and ex-amples only cause perplexion.

More Pictures & Less Text

understandable reference book for "X" should prove to be popular title. It should appeal to programmers of all levels of usage and their experience.

One step down in "scope" from Global are variables that you declare in the General Declarations section of a Form, using the Dim command. These variables will be available to all Controls and Events (or Sub-routines or Functions) which are part of that Form (or Module). However other Forms or Modules cannot access such Form-wide variables or constants.

Variables are like mayflies that live only briefly, do their duty, and then die. Variables created only inside Events pop into existence only when the program is running within that Event, and disappear again as soon as the program goes on to some other Event. The next time the Event is triggered, the variable comes back to life (as a container)—but any value you assigned to it while writing commands within that Event (A$ = "Norman") will be reassigned. If you don't assign a value, the variable is

should prove to be popular title. It should appeal to programmers of all levels of usage and their experience.

The weaknesses of the "X" language's documentation are relative to each customer's background and level of pro-gramming experience. For non-programmers, novices, and, to a lesser extent, prog-rammers unfamiliar with the precursor of the "X" language, the manuals shipped with "X" are too advanced. Difficult concepts are sometimes des-cribed in a confusing way, or only briefly mentioned. Many of the descriptions and ex-amples only cause perplexion.

The weaknesses of the "X" language's documentation are relative to each customer's background and level of pro-gramming experience. For non-programmers, novices, and, to a lesser extent, prog-rammers unfamiliar with the precursor of the "X" language, the manuals shipped with "X" are too advanced. Difficult concepts are sometimes des-cribed in a confusing way, or only briefly mentioned. Many of the descriptions and ex-amples only cause perplexion.

Intermediate and advanced pro-grammers will want far more specific information (and more examples) than the manuals provide. A thorough and understandable reference book for "X" should prove to be popular title. It should appeal to programmers of all levels of usage and their experience.

One step down in "scope" from Global are variables that you declare in the General Declarations section of a Form, using the Dim command. These variables will be available to all Controls and Events (or Sub-routines or Functions) which are part of that Form (or Module). However other Forms or Modules cannot access such Form-wide variables or constants.

manuals shipped with "X" are too advanced. Difficult concepts are sometimes des-cribed in a confusing way, or only briefly mentioned. Many of the descriptions and ex-amples only

should prove to be popular title. It should appeal to programmers of all levels of usage and their experience.

One step down in "scope" from Global are variables that you declare in the General Declarations section of a Form, using the Dim command. These variables will be available to all Controls and Events (or Sub-routines or Functions) which are part of that Form (or Module). However other Forms or Modules cannot access such Form-wide variables or constants.

Variables are like mayflies that live only briefly, do their duty, and then die. Variables created only inside Events pop into existence only when the program is running within that Event, and disappear again as soon as the program goes on to some other Event. The next time the Event is triggered, the variable comes back to life (as a container)—but any value you assigned to it while writing commands within that Event (A$ = "Norman") will be reassigned. If you don't assign a value, the variable is empty.

Longer Stories & Fewer Illustrations

programmers, novices, and, to a lesser extent, prog-rammers unfamiliar with the precursor of the "X" language, the manuals shipped with "X" are too advanced. Difficult concepts are sometimes des-cribed in a confusing way, or only briefly mentioned. Many of the descriptions and ex-amples only cause perplexion.

The weaknesses of the "X" language's documentation are relative to each customer's background and level of pro-gramming experience. For non-programmers, novices, and, to a lesser extent, prog-rammers unfamiliar with the precursor of the "X" language, the manuals shipped with "X" are too advanced. Difficult concepts are sometimes des-cribed in a confusing way, or only briefly mentioned. Many of the descriptions and ex-amples only

Figure 3-15: Regular features in a publication, such as letters to the editor, are sometimes headed with widely spaced letters.

Automatic Kerning

WP also includes an automatic kerning feature. First, select a block of words by pressing Alt-F4. Then turn on the auto-kerning with Shift+F8, 7, 9, 3. The effects will range from acceptable to nonexistent. You probably won't see any effect onscreen (in Page View or Graphics View). You'll have to print the page to see if the automated kerning suits you. Some printers won't support automatic kerning at all; others utilize tables of predefined letter pairs that will be kerned if you turn automatic kerning on. Generally you'll get the best results by leaving automatic kerning off (the default in WP) and kerning by hand as described above. Once you've got some kerning macros, the process is relatively painless and quick anyway.

WORD SPACING

You also don't want to leave big white gaps *between* words, which is one argument against using full justification in narrow columns of text. However, you can adjust word spacing in WP until it suits you (Shift+F8, 7, 9, 6). How can you know if your words are spaced too far apart? Print out a sample, then squint at the page until the text blurs into gray patterns (or turn the page upside down, which should have the same effect). If you can still easily see noticeable gaps between the words, word spacing is too large.

How can you tell if your word spacing is too large?

MOVING ON

Now we've explored many ways to improve a publication by taking care with the words and letters. In the next chapter we'll look at the larger masses of text and white space—margins, columns, text alignment (justification), lines and special effects such as shadowing.

4 Refining the Page

In this chapter we'll explore your options when working with larger sections of text—margins, columns, text alignment (justification), and special effects such as shading, reversing (white type on a black or contrasting background) and initial caps.

Moving out from techniques involving the spacing of individual letters, words lines and paragraphs, we'll consider the space *around* your text. How much white space should you use at the top, bottom and sides of your page?

MARGINS & GUTTERS

You don't want to push your text right to the edges of your pages. Unless you are designing a dictionary or other reference text, you'll want to leave a reasonable margin on all four sides of every page. People will *read* your publication, not look things up in it. And most readers prefer a lighter-looking page. They don't want to be blasted with massed gray text. They want the text framed with white, and they will welcome further lightening with graphics and other design elements.

Figure 4-1: Most publications look best when they're framed with white space.

Figure 4-2: When your margins are too small, the text becomes a gray, somewhat threatening mass.

A second consideration is the *gutter*, the margin where the pages of the document will be bound together. To provide enough binding space, you'll probably need to leave a wider right margin for left-hand pages; for right-hand pages, a larger left margin.

To determine how much extra to leave for the gutter, consider the binding. Will it be "perfect bound," like this book? Then leave about a half-inch extra for the gutter. Or will it be stapled in the center, like many magazines? Are you using a 3-ring binder? If so, you need less gutter. Run a few sample pages through your printer, bind them together and see how they look.

Don't forget to check the gutter.

COLUMNS

A major decision you must make is whether your text will run, from left margin to right margin, across the entire page, like most books, or whether it will flow into columns, like most magazines and newspapers.

Many desktop-published documents are printed out on letter-size paper ($8\frac{1}{2}$ x 11 inches). This size paper is often too narrow for a three-column layout but too wide for a one-column layout. Three narrow columns can make the page look crowded and busy; you also run the risk of having too few words per line or excess hyphenation. On the other hand, if you use a single (page-wide) column, the reader may have trouble retracing from the end of one line to the beginning of the next—unless you double-space the lines.

Because a newspaper page is considerably wider than a book page, newspaper text is normally broken into several vertical columns. It would be difficult for readers to follow a line of text all the way across a newspaper page, and it would be a real feat for the reader to *retrace*, to finish a line and then locate the start of the next line.

Consider your readers when you choose line length.

So your decision about columns should be guided by your page width and the nature and purpose of your publication. The primary reason for using columns is *readability*. Books, brochures, flyers, instruction manuals and letters that are less than 8 inches wide are usually set in a single-column format, not broken into columns. But wider publications—ads, large catalogs, newsletters, menus and other pieces—are often broken into two or more columns. (If you select a very large typeface for an ad, you may not need to use columns, even if the publication is 11 inches wide.)

One excellent solution for brochures, reports and even books is to use two columns, one narrower than the other. Put the text into the wide column, and put comments, subheads or pull-quotes (separated by generous amounts of white space) in the narrow column.

WP allows you to define columns and their widths either before or after you've typed in the text (or imported a text file into a document). Here's an example: start a new document by loading in a text file of your choice (press F5).

The column style we're after is *Parallel* rather than *Newspaper* style. We want the subheads in the outer columns to comment on the text they are parallel to, across from. One way to tell these styles apart: newspaper columns are read down the first column, then up to the top of the second, down the second and so on.

If you type new text into a parallel column, *only the text in that column is forced down the page.* Text in the other, parallel columns is not affected.

Now that you've loaded in a file to practice with, here's how to make parallel columns of uneven width.

> Unequal columns work well with many desktop-published documents.

To Make Uneven Columns

1. Move to the top of the document. Press Home, Home, Up arrow.

2. Press Alt+F7, and choose 1, 1, 3 to select parallel style.

3. Press 2 and type in 2 to create two columns.

4. Press Enter to exit the windows.

Now we'll define the two column widths:

5. Press Alt+F7, select 1, W, E, 1 to edit the width of the first column.

Let's assume the two columns are both currently 3 inches wide, and we want to make the left column 1.5 inches and the right column 4.5 inches, as in Figure 4-3.

Figure 4-3: Exterior subheads (placed in the margin) not only look good; this design is also quite readable.

6. Change the first column's width to 1.5, leave the space between them .5 and change the second column's width to 4.5.

Now exit the menus again.

Note that WP allows you to specify that a column width (or the margin between columns) is *fixed*. Several of WP's commands can cause a column to change widths. If you want to prevent this, turn on the Fixed option when defining column widths.

The "Fixed" option freezes column widths.

If you can view this in Page or Graphics View, you'll see the columns now. If not, try selecting Print Preview from the File menu. If your monitor still won't show the results, you'll have to print a page to see the columns.

To Move Text to the Next Column

Now we only have two columns, and both are filled with text. But we want text in the right column and comments (subheads) in the left column. Move again to the top of the document and press Ctrl+Enter. This moves all the text into the wider column, leaving the narrower column empty and ready for you to type in your subheads. (All codes below the current cursor position also move when you press Ctrl+Enter; it's exactly the same as forcing a page break. In some ways, WP treats separate columns as separate pages.)

To Move Between Columns

How do you move the cursor back to the narrower column? Press Ctrl+Home, Left arrow (or Alt+Left arrow). How about moving back to the wider text column? Press Ctrl+Home, Right arrow (or Alt+Right arrow). If you're using a mouse, just click on the place you want to be. You can move freely around your document, pressing Enter to adjust the spacing of the paragraphs and subheads, then switching to the other column to line things up the way you want them. There are a few additional navigation shortcuts: press Ctrl+Home, End to go to the last column. Press Ctrl+Home, Home, Left arrow to move back to the first column.

By far the most common column style is Newspaper style.

CREATING COLUMNS

In WP you set up columns by placing your cursor where you want the columns to start (or selecting a block of text to make into columns by pressing Alt+F4). Then press Alt+F7, 1, 2. Then type in the number of columns you want. You'll see several choices for column *type*. The default setting (Newspaper) with a between-column spacing of .5 inches works well for most applications.

"Newspaper" is the style most commonly used. It means that you read down one column then start at the top of the next column. "Parallel" is the style used in setting up a table, a list, a book, a script or a spreadsheet—the information can be read up and down or side to side—vertically or horizontally. Parallel columns relate to each other *across* the page. The pages in this book are set in parallel columns, with subheads in the left-hand column and the text they relate to in the adjacent wider column. A TV script will have timing cues in one column; to the right of that will be a column of dialog and narration; and the third, rightmost, column will contain directions about the visuals.

If you select "Block Protect," then when a column becomes so long that it crosses into the next page, it won't split a paragraph into two pieces, one piece on each page. Instead, the entire paragraph will be moved, intact, to the next page, leaving some extra white space on the bottom of the previous page.

If you select "Balanced" Newspaper style, the columns will be aligned across the bottom of the page—both made equally distant from the bottom of the page.

As soon as you select the number of columns you want, you'll notice that you can also select Custom Widths. (Custom Widths remains dimmed and cannot be selected until you've typed in a number higher than one in the Number of Columns box.) The Custom Widths option allows you to build nonsymmetrical columns. Select Custom Widths, then select the Edit option and you can specify your preference for the width of each column.

Two Formulas for Column Width

When determining column width, you want to consider the type size you'll be using, the overall page width and the purpose of the publication. There is an old rule of thumb when determining the "perfect" column width, based on the typeface and point size you're using: type a complete lowercase alphabet, print it, measure the length of the alphabet and multiply by 1.5 to determine the column width.

The lowercase alphabet in the 10-point type size of the Bookman Old Style typeface is exactly 2 inches wide when printed out. So, multiplying this result by 1.5, we come up with 3 inches as the best column width.

In addition to readability, consider your design. Try three columns. Does your page width comfortably divide into multiples of three (including the space you'll want to leave between the columns)? If not, do you want to use a wide outer margin (on the left in left-hand pages, on the right in right-hand pages) to use up the extra odd space? Perhaps you could put subheads in this special margin.

Block Protect keeps sections of your work together when you cross page boundaries.

Try various numbers of columns to see what's readable and appropriate for your design.

And remember, the 1.5 x lowercase alphabet rule isn't hard-and-fast. If you need to use wider columns, you can compensate by increasing the space between words or by increasing the space between lines (the leading).

You could also solve the problem by switching to a different typeface or making the type larger. Ten-point body text is a bit small for many publications; you might want to increase the size to 12-point.

BOOKMAN OLD-STYLE (10 pt.)   abcdefghijklmnopqrstuvwxyz

This column width is too narrow. Words will either have to be frequently hypenated or there will be unsightly spaces inserted to push the longer words onto the next line.

This column is too wide. The eye finds it difficult to move from one line to the next—locating the start of the new text each time a line ends. The lowercase alphabet of ten point Bookman Old-Style type is exactly two inches when printed out so multiplying this result by 1.5 we know that the best column width would be three inches.

This column looks good—and it's easy to read. The eye gets a comfortable chunk of words-per-line and yet can retrace to the next line with no problem. So for this typeface at this point size, three inches is a good column width. Not too narrow (causing a fringe of hypens on the right size), nor too wide, making it tough for readers to keep their place when jumping down a line.

Figure 4-4: Choose a readable column width.

The top column in Figure 4-4 is too narrow. Either many words will have to be hyphenated or there will be unsightly spaces inserted to push the longer words onto the next line.

The next column is too wide. The eye finds it difficult to track all the way back from line ending to line beginning.

The bottom column looks good—and it's easy to read. The eye gets a comfortable block of words per line, yet retracing to the beginning of the next line is no problem. So for this typeface at this point size, 3 inches is a good column width.

Another traditional way to estimate ideal line length is to aim for 57 characters per line. Of course, the many variables in different kinds of publications have much to do with determining ideal line length. Readers of books or technical publications willingly accept longer lines (and longer paragraphs, as well). Newsletters, invitations, flyers and especially advertisements should be designed for easier, more cursory reading. If you do use longer lines, you can add extra space between lines (leading) to improve readability.

If a column is too narrow, hyphenation at line endings will be excessive; too wide, and the reader will have trouble following the text.

TEXT ALIGNMENT

There are two other issues to settle when you use columns— should your text be *flush-left, flush-right, centered* or *justified*? And should you insert a thin line separating the columns? Although full justification (text lines align vertically on the left and on the right) is becoming less common, it is still the choice for most newspapers and magazines.

Choose full justification if you want a formal look.

People often find ragged-right columns easier to read for several reasons. Since there is some leeway in line length, the computer doesn't have to add extra spaces between words. These extra spaces can sometimes be quite large—sometimes only a single, long word appears on a line. All this makes the page look spotty and distracts the eye. Also, full justification increases hyphenation, and split words are always a distraction, a grave interruption of the thinking process.

People often find ragged-right columns easier to read for several reasons. Since there is some leeway in line length, the computer doesn't have to add extra spaces between words. These extra spaces can sometimes be quite large—sometimes only a single, long word appears on a line. All this makes the page look spotty and distracts the eye. Also, full justification increases hyphenation, and split words are always a distraction, a grave interruption of the thinking process.

Figure 4-5: Fully justified columns look more formal than columns with flush-left/ragged-right alignment.

The fully justified top column in Figure 4-5 looks conservative and dignified. If you choose ragged-right columns, as shown in the lower example in Figure 4-5, you'll get a less "official" look, and that's often the choice for more informal or *energetic* pieces such as advertisements, newsletters, menus, catalogs, signs, flyers and brochures.

In WP, you select the kind of alignment (left, centered, right, full justification or full *all lines* justification) by pressing Shift-F8 and selecting 1. The Full All Lines option means that no matter how r i d i c u l o u s it looks, spaces will be inserted between *letters* if necessary to achieve a right-hand alignment. (This happens at the end of paragraphs where a word or two is s t r e t c h e d to fill the final line.) This makes text particularly painful to read and should be avoided, even in headlines.

People often find ragged-right columns easier to read, for several reasons. Since there is some leeway in line length, the computer doesn't have to add extra spaces between words. In fully justified lines, these extra spaces can sometimes be quite large—sometimes only a single, long word appears on

Text with an unjustified right margin is often easier to read.

a line. This makes a page look spotty and distracts the reader. Another advantage in using flush-left/ragged-right alignment is that the need for hyphenation—always a distraction and interruption to the thinking process—decreases considerably. Finally, when lines are irregular in length, the eye can more easily find its place when leaving the end of one line and locating the start of the next line. However, if the text comes out *too* ragged to suit you, you can fiddle with word spacing and character spacing settings (Shift+F8, 7, 9, 6), or hyphenate some words to even things out.

Pros & Cons

There are two primary advantages of full justification. It lends a kind of *credibility* and *authority* to the text. Although the pages tend to look more stiff and more gray, fully justified type is still widely used, perhaps for the same reason that suits and ties are still thought essential to convey sufficient *gravitas* if one is employed in certain professions. Indoors, a suit coat is usually unnecessary and often too hot. A tie firmly secured around the neck is all too reminiscent of a leash. Nevertheless, studies have shown that men so attired are more likely to be trusted.

The second advantage of full justification is that it saves money. You can print the same amount of information in fewer pages. But this second advantage doesn't apply when you justify in WordPerfect, unless your columns are quite wide or you adjust the "justification limits." The reason is that WP, like most word processors, doesn't perform true justification by default. Truly justified text is achieved by adding (*and subtracting*) space between words *and between letters* (kerning).

In the old days (before 1960) most text was typeset pretty much the way it had been for hundreds of years—each line was built up of metal letters and metal spaces. When done by hand, justification could be achieved via subtle adjustments to the letters within the text. True justification is attractive and relatively easy to read.

However, in its default setting, the only adjustment WP makes is to *add space between words* in order to make the right side of a column line up. This is a relatively crude tactic and results in "rivers of white" that snake down between lines and annoy the reader. For one thing, these patterns of white cause the brain to flicker between the zone in your head that reads words and the entirely separate zone that recognizes graphic patterns. Added to this subliminal, but quite real, annoyance, all this extra padding with white space cancels the cost saving of eliminating white space at the ends of lines.

Like most word processors, WP makes some compromises when it justifies, unless you set justification limits.

To make full justification look as good as possible within narrow columns, press Shift+F8, 7, 9, 1. You'll see the default limits: squeeze 60 percent or expand 400 percent. Our goal is to make the word spacing limits narrower—forcing WP to adjust letter spacing instead. Change to 30 compression and 100 expansion. Even then, WP can still double the word spacing from its natural limit—and this can still create rivers of white. A further improvement can be made by setting hyphenation *on*. To do this: Shift+F8, 1, 6.

But after all this effort, you still might find rivers running through it. If so, the only good solution is to either turn justification off or make your column wider.

COLUMN RULES

Separating columns with a rule is no longer necessary.

Putting a line (a *rule)* or other separator between columns has become uncommon these days. Like full justification, column rules give your page a formal, somewhat antique look. Nonetheless, WP offers many styles of rules to choose from—thin or fat, dotted or dashed, various shades of gray.

Press Alt+F7, 1, 5 (Column Borders). You'll see three options: 1. Border Style 2. Fill Style 3. Customize. If you choose Border Style, the menu in Figure 4-6 appears. As you can see, there is a generous set of choices, but column rules are almost always thin solid lines between columns. You probably won't use column rules very often, but when you do, you'll probably select Between Only.

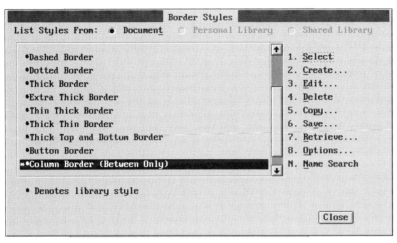

Figure 4-6: The default option, Column Border (Between Only), is almost always the one you'll use.

In keeping with the fact that you can always ignore options—but when you need them you really do need them—WP as usual provides you considerable flexibility. You can select from the many choices shown in Figure 4-7 by pressing Alt+F7, 1, 5, 3.

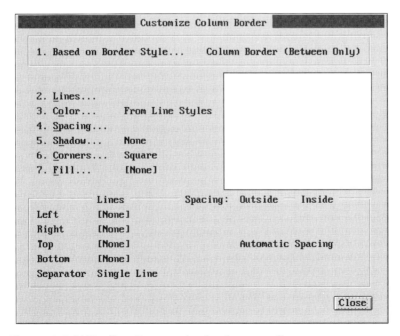

Figure 4-7: WP offers lines and rules in many flavors.

If you select the WP default options (Alt+F7, 1, 5, 1), WP will automatically create and space the standard thin column rule illustrated in Figure 4-8.

There are many ways to use rules to improve your pages.

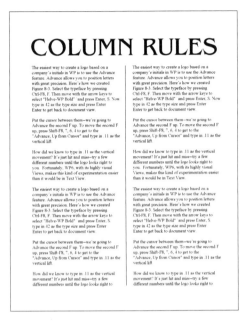

Figure 4-8: A conventional column rule lends formality to a page.

Rules, however, are not limited to simply dividing columns. You can place these lines on your page to assist the reader (organizing the text into various sections) or to add variety and visual excitement to the design. We'll look next at rules used for *graphic* purposes, along with several other special effects you might want to use to make your piece more attractive visually.

SPECIAL EFFECTS

Rules, sinks, initial caps, bleeds, shadows, reverses and screens are special effects and transformations that can be achieved in WP 6.0. There is also WP's Image Editor. (Because the Image Editor is so useful, we'll cover it in detail in Chapter 7.) However, there are a number of graphic effects available in WP's graphics menu and its submenus. One important effect is adding lines to your page.

RULES

Lines—thick or thin, horizontal or vertical—are called *rules*, and need not be used merely to separate columns. Rules can also be employed in design.

Figure 4-9: A rule under a full-length headline often looks attractive, particularly if you include some white space near it.

One of the most common uses for horizontal rules is to add weight to a headline. If you think of the headline vs. the gray body copy as a problem of page *balance*, the head has greater weight because it's darker, but the body text has more mass. Adding a line beneath the head serves to separate it graphically from the text and also give it more weight. There's no mathematical formula for calculating gray mass vs. black headline, but most people would agree that the right-hand page in Figure 4-9 is more pleasing and more harmonic than the left-hand version.

Figure 4-9 also illustrates another technique: making the thickness of the rule roughly the same as the thickness of the letters in the headline.

Horizontal rules can also be used to divide a page into logical sections. In Figure 4-10 two rules set off a table of contents for a newsletter. Note that we use two columns of text but leave the left column blank except for a single graphic—an illustration of a vegetable. (Using extra white space is common in modern design; it gives the page "air" and "lightness.")

Is this in balance? By making the table of contents text fairly large, and by including the rule and the graphic, we counterbalance the weight of the gray mass of text in the other two columns. If we put a photograph into the white space, however, we might tilt the balance to the left side of this page and throw it out of whack. You just want to use your eye, putting in rules, graphics or white space (and moving them around) until you feel that the page balances.

Surround special sections of your page with rules.

Figure 4-10: Horizontal rules can embrace a table of contents.

Another common use for horizontal rules is to set off a pull-quote or sidebar. Pull-quotes are short quotations taken out of the main text to intrigue the reader about the content of an article. Pull-quotes are frequently seen in magazines but are still fairly rare in newspapers.

However, both magazines and newspapers are using sidebars more and more these days. A sidebar is a short section of text which is related, but supplementary, to the main article. For example, an article on Nome, Alaska, might have a sidebar on "Nome's Best Restaurants." Pull-quotes are almost always set off by horizontal rules, but sidebars are usually put into boxes. Nonetheless, a short sidebar, like the one in Figure 4-11, can look good set off by horizontal rules rather than stuffed into a small box.

Use rules to set off pull-quotes and sidebars.

Figure 4-11: Use rules to set off a sidebar.

SINKS

A *sink*, or *drop*, is a deep top margin on a page. A fairly large upper margin can open up your design and is currently a raging fashion in page design. Just be sure that your sinks *are the same on every page* of your publication.

Keep your sinks equal throughout the whole document.

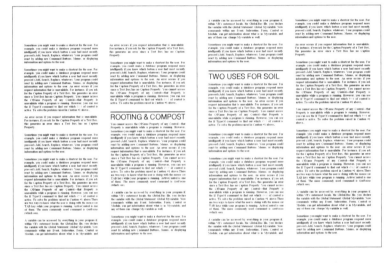

Figure 4-12: A sink adds white space at the top and makes your pages look less threatening to the reader. But avoid uneven sinks like these.

Notice that the drops in Figure 4-12 are not equal. Unless the page on the left is the start of an article *and you include a headline*, the different-sized top margins break up the flow of your design. They just don't look right. But compare the pages in Figure 4-13: which set of pages is more inviting?

Although your sinks (like all margins) should be the same from page to page, it's also a good idea to sometimes invade the sink with a photo or other graphic. Like other space violations, this adds depth and dimension to your work.

Figure 4-13: Don't hesitate to "invade" a sink with a graphic. The curved-letter logo used here was made in CorelDRAW then imported into WP. (Clip Art from CorelDRAW)

INITIAL CAPS

First used centuries ago as decoration, initial caps (or *drop caps*) are still used to add variety or balance to a document. Initial caps can also alert the reader that something—an article, a section, a paragraph—is *starting*. In other words, just like headlines and subheads, initial caps can provide the reader with signposts, showing divisions between the sections or zones of your publication.

Drop caps can make a page look slightly formal (especially if you use a serif typeface). If you don't want to use a drop cap, consider alternatives such as using (in the first line or first paragraph of your article) a larger type size with more space (leading) between the lines. Another substitute for drop caps is setting the whole first paragraph in small caps. You can also consider reversing a drop cap (a white letter on a black background). (To find out how to reverse text or graphics, see "Reverses" later in this chapter.)

Another typical strategy to draw attention to the start of an article is to make the first few words all-caps.

There are several alternatives to drop caps.

But if you want to use initial caps, there are several ways to add them. One style puts the large cap out into the margin. Another style flows the text around the capitalized letter. You can simulate one variety of initial caps by a little fiddling with letter- and line-spacing adjustments.

In Figure 4-14, we first selected the W, then changed its point size. The rest of the text is 12-point, but we enlarged the W to 30 points (Ctrl+F8). Notice, however, that this moves the rest of the text, the *hen* etc., over to the right on that top line. It also creates an extra space between the first line and the second line. WP is making space for that big W.

W hen determining column width, you want to consider type size, page width and the purpose of the publication. There is an old rule of thumb which is based on the typeface and point size you're using: type a complete lowercase alphabet, print it, measure it and multiply the result by 1.5

W hen determining column width, you want to consider type size, page width and the purpose of the publication. There is an old rule of thumb which is based on the typeface and point size you're using: type a complete lowercase alphabet, print it, measure it and multiply the result by 1.5

Figure 4-14: WP can simulate initial caps.

To make this odd spacing less odd, first move the cursor to just in front of the W to adjust letter spacing (Shift+F8, 7, 9, 6, 2, 3). Then reduce the letter spacing to 65 percent or whatever setting brings the *hen* up tight underneath the W. Exit the menus by pressing Enter repeatedly. Move the cursor in front of the *hen* to restore normal letter spacing (Shift+F8, 7, 9, 6, 2, 3 again) and select 100 percent (Optimal).

Auto Code Placement

Next we want to reduce the line spacing between the first and second lines. However, WP sends certain control codes, including line spacing, to the start of a paragraph. We want to put one line-space code at the start of the paragraph, then move down to the second line to make another adjustment that will govern the rest of the document. To prevent WP from moving our codes to the start of the paragraph, we need to turn Auto Code Placement on or off: press Shift+F1, 3, T.

At the time of this writing, WP's Auto Code Placement is working backwards—when on, it *doesn't* auto-place. Perhaps it will have been corrected by the time you read this. If you cannot get the line spacing that we describe below to work, change the setting of Auto Code Placement and you'll be able to insert two line-spacing commands within a single paragraph, which is our intention.

Put your cursor in front of the large W and press Shift+F8, 1, 3, then select .75 or whatever looks best. How much to reduce line spacing will depend on your particular character, typeface and type size. In Figure 4-14, we used .78. The results aren't ideal, but it's an improvement. Your goal should be to reduce the space between the first and second lines without causing the descenders (the strokes in letters such as p and g that descend below some letters on the line) of the characters in the first line to be cut off by the ascenders (the strokes that rise, such as in the letters b and d) in the second line. Now, to make the rest of the text properly spaced, again press Shift+F8, 1, 3, then select .85 or whatever looks good.

It's important to fix bad line spacing.

Toggle WP's Auto Code Placement switch if you get unexpected results.

BLEEDS

Figure 4-15: When text or a graphic extends off the page, this effect is called a bleed.

A bleed can be text, a rule, a graphic—something that is incompletely visible (only part of the object is on the page). Like other "dimensional effects," bleeds have become increasingly fashionable, particularly in advertising where you want to suggest that the product just *explodes* beyond normal boundaries. But bleeds can also create other interesting graphic effects—when you use them with some restraint.

WP doesn't allow you to drag a graphic image beyond the borders of the page. However, you can achieve the effect of a bleed by *cropping* (trimming) an image or text character in a graphics program such as CorelDRAW or Arts & Letters. Just create the image you want, then select a portion of that image—as if the image were flowing off a page. You can also crop using the Image Editor (see Chapter 7).

In Figure 4-15, we took a bicycle silhouette, lopped off the left and top of the image, and saved it as a graphics file (.PCX in this case).

Then, we have to go through several steps to position this graphic in a WP document. First, import the image into a document (Shift+F10). Then, go into the graphics menus (Alt+F9) and, to remove the default box around the graphic, press 1, 2, Enter, 6, 2, 1, 1, and select None. Now that the box is gone, we want to position the graphic. Press Enter, Enter to get back to the main menu, then press 7 and select Attach To Page. Now press 8, 3, None, to allow the graphic to bleed off to the upper left of the page. If you have a mouse, you can move the graphic to the upper left of the page.

The same technique—cropping, then retrieving the graphic, then positioning at an extreme edge of the page—can be used to bleed characters, photos, etc.

SHADOWS

In the real, three-dimensional world we live in, there are almost always shadows—places where objects interrupt the flow of the strongest local light sources. WP allows you to add shadows to Graphics Boxes and lettering. Needless to say, adding a shadow makes an object appear more three-dimensional, makes it appear to move toward the viewer and to be somewhat lifted off the page.

Use Shadows for . . .
SPECIAL EFFECTS

Figure 4-16: WP's text and Graphics Box shadowing effects.

You can choose the percentage of shading for boxes but not text.

You cannot select the shade or positioning of shadows for text, although you can select the shade for Graphics Box shadows. Notice in Figure 4-16 that we have turned on the shadowing for the text (Ctrl+F8), and that shade (about 50 percent black) is the only possible one for lettering in WP. Likewise, the positioning is fixed by WP and cannot be adjusted by you (the distance the shadow falls from the text creates the illusion of how far up from the background the letters are thrust toward the reader). Note also in Figure 4-16 that our Graphics Box is shadowed, but we have adjusted the shade (from the default, 100 percent black, to 25 percent black). You adjust the shade of a Graphics Box's shadow by pressing Alt+F9, 1, 6, 5, 2.

If you want some percentage other than 100 percent black, you should stay with standard increments, such as 75 percent, 50 percent or 25 percent. Most printers (and video monitors, too) have a hard time creating a smooth effect with odd percentages of black. You want to avoid strange-looking patterns that can result when the printer attempts to simulate an in-between shade.

Instead of good grays, you might get dithers.

This simulation is called *dithering*, and it occurs when your monitor or printer is not capable of producing more than 2, 16 or 64 shades of gray (or a limited number of colors). Since there are 100 shades of gray you could use for a shadow, clearly some of them will fall outside the range of smooth reproduction if your printer is limited to 64 or fewer shades. (You need not worry about this if your printer is able to produce 256 shades or more.) When the computer is faced with a shade of gray that is not in its available set, it *dithers* and produces a pattern of black or white spots. If you are viewing it from far enough away that you don't see the patterns, this effect is mitigated enough to be acceptable. Unfortunately, readers will not be far enough away.

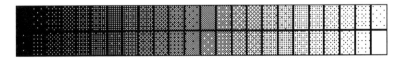

Figure 4-17: Try to avoid dithering, the odd pattern your printer produces in a vain attempt to create in-between gray shades.

Dithering

Figure 4-17 shows various kinds of dithering. In this case, we have a two-color image. So black and white are the only pure colors in the palette. In between, there are 46 simulated shades of gray. Of them, only a few of the dithers look even reasonably smooth (see the boxes located at about 25 percent, 50 percent and 75 percent), but even they look like the pattern on a cheap suit of clothes. Moral: avoid dithering whenever possible. If necessary, use 100 percent black, even though it's a rather unnatural look (because such a strong shadow would occur only in the dead of night when a single light bulb is turned on).

Interestingly, although you cannot adjust the shade of text shadowing, you *can* adjust the shade, and color, of the text itself (Ctrl+F8, C Color, 2 Shade).

Figure 4-16 demonstrates that the light source (where the strongest light is located) is set by WP in the upper left. Therefore, the shadow is cast to the lower right of the text or graphic. This WP default light-source/shadow position is also the one most commonly used in publications and computer graphics. The shadowing of WP's own Graphics View likewise follows this upper-left-light-source rule (see the raised slider and exit button in Figure 4-6 or any program running in Windows).

You can choose the color of the text but not the color of its shadow.

Drop Shadows

Shadows, sometimes called *drop shadows*, are particularly effective for titles of publications and for some illustrations and photos. They can add an almost holographic realism to your page. Since WP's shadowing facilities are relatively limited, you might want to create a shadow effect in a drawing program like CorelDRAW, Arts & Letters or PaintBrush (see the Resource List for supplementary software sources). When you've created your shadowed title or graphic, just "retrieve" it into your page as a graphic, place it where you want it, and remove the Graphics Box border that WP automatically inserts around any retrieved graphic. Here's how:

We not only want to make a shadow that's distinctly separate from the title of our Fishing is Fun booklet, but we also

Angled and foreshortened shadows create a dramatic effect.

want the shadow line to be tilted at an angle, quite light and *shorter* than the original line. Try to imagine where the light source would have to be in order to create this dramatic effect, where the left side of the title seems closer to the page than the right side.

Figure 4-18: You can shorten, lighten and tilt shadows using a drawing program (WP can't produce these effects).

The first thing we do is select one of CorelDRAW's fonts and type in our title, *Fishing is Fun!* Then we rotate the title to the desired angle and use CorelDRAW's *duplicate* feature to make a copy. We position the copy below and behind the original, then turn it until it's almost horizontal, and fill it with a light-gray shade.

At this point we use the Edit envelope feature, which allows us to foreshorten and distort the shape of the text somewhat. The same effect is created with the fishing pole and fish. Finally, the entire graphic is saved from CorelDRAW as a .PCX graphics file (which WP can retrieve when you press

Shift+F10). Then, go into the WP graphics menus (Alt+F9) and, to remove the default box around the graphic, press 1, 2, Enter, 6, 2, 1, 1, and select None.

REVERSES

A *reverse* is a negative image: white text against a black or contrasting background. A reversed headline attracts the eye (more than other, normal headlines on the page). A reversed graphic can look like an X-ray or create somewhat ghostly special effects. As with other effects—like italics, boxes, rules or decorative typefaces—think of reverses as a spice to be used with discretion. Reverse too many headlines and they compete with each other for attention so that the primary value of the reverse technique (its ability to draw attention) is defeated. What's more, with too many reverses, your page looks too busy—like a checkerboard.

Go easy on reversing text or you'll end up with a checkerboard effect.

Figure 4-19: WP allows you to reverse images and text.

One hint to remember when reversing headlines: they are almost always more readable and look better if you use a sans-serif font like Univers and leave some black space around the lettering. In Figure 4-19, compare the BIG SALE headline set in the generous background to the cramped version set in a much smaller box.

To reverse text, there are several nested menus to access. As is usual with a multimenu process, it's easier to create a macro. Macros automate otherwise tedious processes. In effect, a macro gives you a new command which is easily accessed and almost instantly accomplishes what you might spend several minutes doing in a long sequence of keystroke or menu selections. We've included such a macro, called "REVERSE.WPM," on the companion disk for this book. We'll go into techniques for creating and modifying macros in more depth in Chapter 6.

When you want to reverse a headline, press Alt+F9 and select 1, 1, 6, 7, 1, then move the cursor to "100% fill." Then press Enter, Enter, Enter to get back to the first menu. Select 3 (Create Text). Select a font in the usual way. In Figure 4-19 we selected Univers Bold at 30 pts.

Now select Color for the text, select White and press 1 for Select. Now choose 3 for Create Text and type in your headline (it will be white-on-white at this point, so you won't see it). Then press F7 to exit and close all the menus.

Placing a Headline

The headline will probably not be placed exactly where you want it, nor will the black space be large enough for good readability. So, at this point, we want to size and position the Graphics Box. With a mouse it's simple: just click on the headline and drag the box where you want it on the page (as long as you have selected the Attach To Page option in the Graphics Box editing window). To do the same thing via the keyboard: Alt+F9, 1, 2, Enter, 9, 2, and select Set for both position (8) and size (9) of the box. You'll have to experiment a little (going into the menus and back to the clean screen to see the effects of your adjustments). If you select the Automatic Based On Contents option, you'll probably find that the black space is too small around the text.

To reverse a graphic, the process is similar. In Figure 4-19 we chose the TREE.WPG illustration that comes with WP. Let's assume that you've "Retrieved" that or some other im-

Reversing text
is quicker and
easier if you
use macros.

Reversing
graphics is
similar to
reversing text.

age into your page (Shift+F10). Now, to reverse it, double-click on the image with the mouse, or use Alt+F9, 1, 2, 1, then select the number of the Graphics Box you want to edit. Boxes are numbered in the order that you create them, and WP inserts the number of the most recently created box. You can change this number to select a different box if the default number is not what you want. Now, press 1, 6, 7, 1, and select "100%." Then press 1, and if the background color isn't set to White, change it so that it is. Now close all boxes and you'll see your reversed graphic (you may have to save your document before you can see the effect).

Inverting

A shortcut is to select Invert in the Image Editor. We'll explore the WP Image Editor thoroughly in Chapter 7. However, you can press Alt+F9, 1, 2, select the correct box, then Enter, 3, i to invert an image quickly. Note that if the image is in color, you'll get a color inversion instead of a true negative. You might, therefore, want to first select the "B&W" option ("b") to get a cleaner result. Color inversion is unpredictable—for example, it can change blue to yellow, red to green and vice versa. The printed result, unless you are printing in color, can look substantially like the original—with only grays, blacks and whites actually inverted while the colors remain the same shade (the colors were inverted, but when printed in black, white and gray on a printer, the *color* inversion might not show up).

The Image Editor offers a quick way to create a reverse.

SCREENS

Like reverses, screens add a special background to text—but screens are less drastic than reverses. Screens can add variety to your pages and draw attention to special sections such as tables of contents. A screen is a shaded gray background behind text. You can select the amount of shading (the percent of black) for the screen and for the text that is placed on top of the screen.

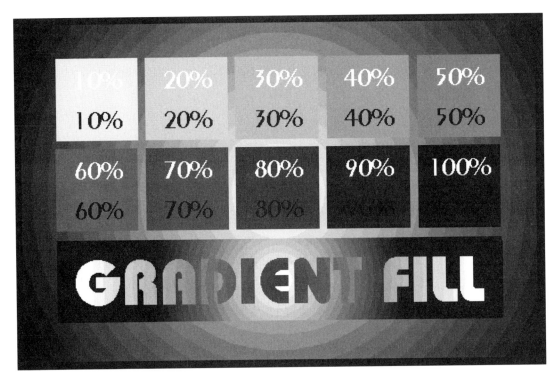

Figure 4-20: The effects of various background shades.

BENEFITS OF A DRAWING PROGRAM

Think about supplementing WP with a drawing/ retouching program.

If you are going to be putting out a variety of publications, you might want to consider investing in a drawing/retouching program such as CorelDRAW. Although WP includes many useful text and graphics manipulation features, you can add many additional tools to your design toolbox with CorelDRAW. It does require Windows, but working with graphics is what Windows was created for, and you'll find your options considerably increased if you add these facilities to WP. (Other graphics programs—including Arts & Letters and DeluxePaint—are also worth considering.)

WP makes it easy to import graphics. All you need to do is retrieve a graphic, then remove the box that WP, by default, draws around any imported graphic. You can't tell that the importation wasn't part of the original page designed in WP. And you give yourself many new options this way.

Figure 4-21: Among many other CorelPHOTO-PAINT techniques is one that lets you *blur*, creating an underwater effect.

The *gradient* (or radial) fill shown at the bottom and in the background in Figures 4-20 and 4-21 was created in CorelDRAW. Circular and linear shading are only two of the background options you can select in CorelDRAW. WP also allows you to create gradient and radial fills. The results, however, include considerable dithering (roughness). Here's how: Press Alt+F9, 1, 1, 6, 7, 1, 2. Name it "bullseye," press 1 and select Gradient. Press 4, 1, and select linear, radial or rectangular (diamond-shaped shading).

Figure 4-22: In WordPerfect, you can vary the shade of both the background and the foreground text.

MOVING ON

Now that we've covered the main elements of design, let's look at the pitfalls, the things you should check before actually publishing. In the next chapter, we'll start with several common problems (including some with uncommon names like *tombstones* and *orphans*) then move on to more general issues like contrast, variety and taste. After you've cast a cold, impartial eye on your work, and made any necessary last-minute adjustments, your publication should look polished, professional and inviting. This process of polishing is usually best left until after you've finished the layout and design. If you can let the project sit for a few days without looking at it, all the better.

This final scrutiny should be as objective as possible. Your final polishing should be to page design what editing is to writing: taking a good look at what's been done *through the objective eyes of a reader*. If you can check out your work as if you'd never seen it before, you're more likely to spot things that could be improved.

Some polishing (looking for crowding or for dangling words, for example) is merely a matter of knowing what to look for and is often quite simple to correct. Other things, such as taste and appropriateness, are more abstract and subjective, often harder for you to spot and sometimes harder to correct. Nevertheless, a final "ruthless" appraisal of your work can mean the difference between a clumsy, amateurish design and one you can be proud of.

Look at your work through a reader's eye.

5 Taking a Second Look

Before you desktop publish a piece of work, take a break. Then print it out and look at it as if you were a reader, seeing it for the first time. One approach is to check the details: search for widows and orphans, tombstones, crowding, inappropriate typefaces, badly designed headlines, etc. (We'll define all these terms shortly.)

Take a break, then look at your work "for the first time."

Then, when you've cleaned up these problems, ask the big questions: Does the design make you want to read it? Is it inviting to the reader? Is there enough contrast and variety? Is it tasteful yet stimulating? Is the look appropriate to the topic?

Of course, you should ask these big questions in the early stages of creating your design. But this final checklist is where you can make sure you've achieved your goals. It's not too late to make revisions. With WP, even some major revisions, such as changing typefaces, moving boxes and adding rules, can be accomplished relatively quickly.

IT'S IN THE DETAILS

Avoid giving the reader a puzzle.

An author will seem less credible if his or her writing contains misspellings, bad punctuation or poor grammar. These are details, but they are important details. Similarly, a publication containing widows, free-floating headlines or unreadable captions will discourage readers. People don't mind puzzles when they're in the mood, but they resent puzzles that derive from sloppiness on your part.

Incorrect spelling or punctuation can create a puzzle, stopping the reader and requiring a few moments to make a translation. A single sentence is bad enough, but keep this up across paragraphs and pages and you'll soon lose your reader. Most readers just won't take the time to translate your puzzling and unique spelling into English they can understand. Nor will readers be willing to endure graphic sloppiness—hard-to-read typefaces, crowded headlines, too many boxes, whatever.

In this chapter we're going to examine the most common flaws in desktop publishing design. In each case we'll state the problem—showing you what to look for—then suggest solutions. There are almost always several ways to solve design problems, so your imagination and common sense may lead you to an even better solution.

Use both common sense and imagination when polishing your work.

WIDOWS & ORPHANS

When a column ends with a short line, it's called a widow. This is considered poor design and should be eliminated by you.

The Widow

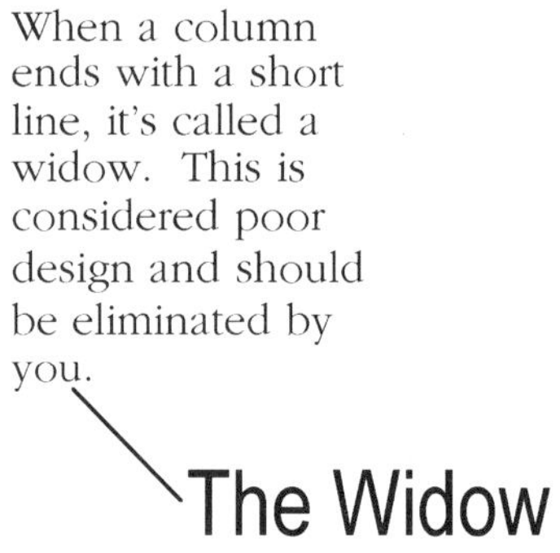

Figure 5-1: A *widow* is a too-short line at the end of a column.

The Orphan

more.
Columns that start with
a short line are not pretty.
So you should try to get
rid of any orphans you
find in your text after the
text has been formatted.

Figure 5-2: An *orphan* is a too-short line at the start of a column.

Problem: Your page will look visually rough if you include a column that starts or ends with a line less than half as long as the rest of the lines in the column. Orphans tend to look worse than widows; both are distracting but usually easy to fix. Like a thread dangling off someone's pants or a piece of toilet paper stuck to a shoe, they look untidy and attract the eye for no good reason. You want to control where your readers' eyes go, not distract them with visual debris.

Solution: Either you or the writer should edit the text. That's the easiest fix. Adding a word somewhere in the same paragraph, or taking out a word or two, should solve the problem. For example, in Figure 5-1 we could get rid of the widow by changing *eliminated by you* to *fixed.* If editing text doesn't work, adjust other elements of the page, such as paragraph spacing, to eliminate the offending extra bit of text. More space between paragraphs should force a widow up to the next column or page. Thinner spacing will bring an orphan back. (To change paragraph spacing in WP: Shift+F8, 2, 8 will adjust paragraph spacing from the default 1 to 1.7 or whatever, to thicken the space. To bring the paragraphs closer together, choose .75, or whatever fraction less than 1 looks right.)

Editing text is the easiest way to get rid of widows and orphans.

A second solution is to let WP eliminate widows and orphans for you: go to the top of your document (Home, Home, Up arrow), then turn on Widow and Orphan Protect (press Shift+F8, 7, 3). This can, however, result in some odd-looking spacing as WP tries to fix the problem.

For the best-looking results, you might be better off editing the text yourself rather than having WP do it automatically.

TOMBSTONES

Tombstones result from too much symmetry in your design.

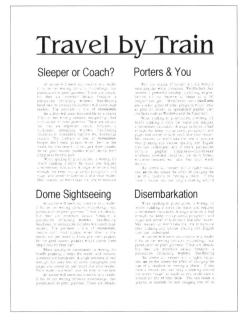

Figure 5-3: When subheads line up across columns, the result looks like a row of *tombstones.*

Problem: When your columns and subheads line up across the page, you've got a case of excess symmetry. The result looks like tombstones in a church yard (see Figure 5-3). Readers can get confused and read two single adjacent heads as one, as if the page were organized horizontally instead of vertically (as the columns imply).

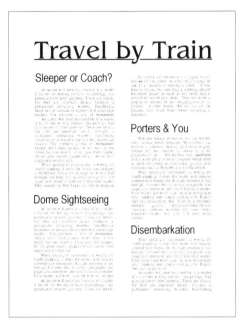

Figure 5-4: Stagger your subheads to avoid tombstones.

Solution: Add or subtract some text, change the typeface or type size, move a subhead to a new location, or take some other action that will stagger the subheads. You want your subheads to help organize sections of your text. To do this, they must be placed at irregular intervals—not lined up side by side on the page.

GRAY PAGES

Problem: Trying to fit too much on a page is false efficiency. Readers don't like gray pages with only small slivers of white space. You want people to *read* what you publish, so don't try to save paper by cramming things together. You'll end up wasting the paper if they toss your work away unread.

Modern readers dislike gray pages; some would say we're spoiled by too much "graphic relief."

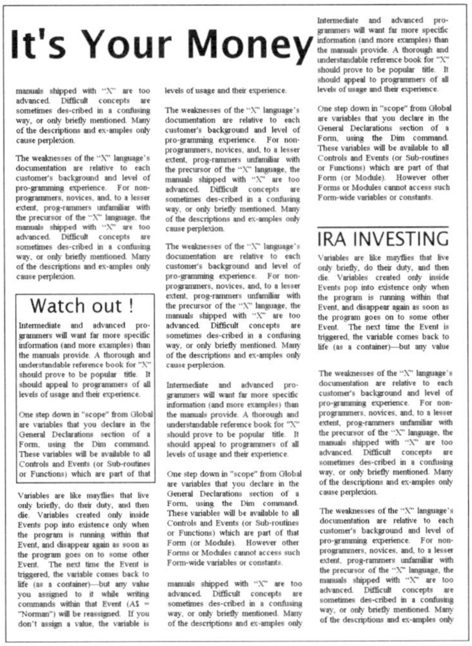

It's Your Money

manuals shipped with "X" are too advanced. Difficult concepts are sometimes des-cribed in a confusing way, or only briefly mentioned. Many of the descriptions and ex-amples only cause perplexion.

The weaknesses of the "X" language's documentation are relative to each customer's background and level of pro-gramming experience. For non-programmers, novices, and, to a lesser extent, prog-rammers unfamiliar with the precursor of the "X" language, the manuals shipped with "X" are too advanced. Difficult concepts are sometimes des-cribed in a confusing way, or only briefly mentioned. Many of the descriptions and ex-amples only cause perplexion.

Watch out !

Intermediate and advanced pro-grammers will want far more specific information (and more examples) than the manuals provide. A thorough and understandable reference book for "X" should prove to be popular title. It should appeal to programmers of all levels of usage and their experience.

One step down in "scope" from Global are variables that you declare in the General Declarations section of a Form, using the Dim command. These variables will be available to all Controls and Events (or Sub-routines or Functions) which are part of that

Variables are like mayflies that live only briefly, do their duty, and then die. Variables created only inside Events pop into existence only when the program is running within that Event, and disappear again as soon as the program goes on to some other Event. The next time the Event is triggered, the variable comes back to life (as a container)—but any value you assigned to it while writing commands within that Event (A$ = "Norman") will be reassigned. If you don't assign a value, the variable is

levels of usage and their experience.

The weaknesses of the "X" language's documentation are relative to each customer's background and level of pro-gramming experience. For non-programmers, novices, and, to a lesser extent, prog-rammers unfamiliar with the precursor of the "X" language, the manuals shipped with "X" are too advanced. Difficult concepts are sometimes des-cribed in a confusing way, or only briefly mentioned. Many of the descriptions and ex-amples only cause perplexion.

The weaknesses of the "X" language's documentation are relative to each customer's background and level of pro-gramming experience. For non-programmers, novices, and, to a lesser extent, prog-rammers unfamiliar with the precursor of the "X" language, the manuals shipped with "X" are too advanced. Difficult concepts are sometimes des-cribed in a confusing way, or only briefly mentioned. Many of the descriptions and ex-amples only cause perplexion.

Intermediate and advanced pro-grammers will want far more specific information (and more examples) than the manuals provide. A thorough and understandable reference book for "X" should prove to be popular title. It should appeal to programmers of all levels of usage and their experience.

One step down in "scope" from Global are variables that you declare in the General Declarations section of a Form, using the Dim command. These variables will be available to all Controls and Events (or Sub-routines or Functions) which are part of that Form (or Module). However other Forms or Modules cannot access such Form-wide variables or constants.

manuals shipped with "X" are too advanced. Difficult concepts are sometimes des-cribed in a confusing way, or only briefly mentioned. Many of the descriptions and ex-amples only

Intermediate and advanced pro-grammers will want far more specific information (and more examples) than the manuals provide. A thorough and understandable reference book for "X" should prove to be popular title. It should appeal to programmers of all levels of usage and their experience.

One step down in "scope" from Global are variables that you declare in the General Declarations section of a Form, using the Dim command. These variables will be available to all Controls and Events (or Sub-routines or Functions) which are part of that Form (or Module). However other Forms or Modules cannot access such Form-wide variables or constants.

IRA INVESTING

Variables are like mayflies that live only briefly, do their duty, and then die. Variables created only inside Events pop into existence only when the program is running within that Event, and disappear again as soon as the program goes on to some other Event. The next time the Event is triggered, the variable comes back to life (as a container)—but any value

The weaknesses of the "X" language's documentation are relative to each customer's background and level of pro-gramming experience. For non-programmers, novices, and, to a lesser extent, prog-rammers unfamiliar with the precursor of the "X" language, the manuals shipped with "X" are too advanced. Difficult concepts are sometimes des-cribed in a confusing way, or only briefly mentioned. Many of the descriptions and ex-amples only cause perplexion.

The weaknesses of the "X" language's documentation are relative to each customer's background and level of pro-gramming experience. For non-programmers, novices, and, to a lesser extent, prog-rammers unfamiliar with the precursor of the "X" language, the manuals shipped with "X" are too advanced. Difficult concepts are sometimes des-cribed in a confusing way, or only briefly mentioned. Many of the descriptions and ex-amples only

Figure 5-5: There's too little space around text and headlines here.

Solution: Spread the work over enough pages to allow sufficient white space so your work is easy to read and its organization is clear.

HEADLINE PLACEMENT

Problem: A subhead should be near the text block it belongs to. But it shouldn't be only two or three lines from the bottom of a page.

Headlines look like widows, too.

Figure 5-6: The upper left subhead isn't clearly attached to the text below it and the lower left subhead is too close to the bottom of the page.

Solution: Move the subhead down against the text it describes. (In Figure 5-6, the only headline that's correctly placed is "Porters & You.") To solve the bottom-of-the-page problem, add some text, change margins, change typeface size or do whatever it takes to avoid this "widow headline" that seems to overwhelm the two lines of text.

TYPEWRITER EFFECTS

If your publication looks like it was typewritten, many people won't take it seriously.

Figure 5-7: You should transform A, the summer camp amateur newsletter look, into B, a professional typeset appearance.

Problem: If your work looks typewritten or mimeographed, it will look amateurish. Most people are still taught typing on a typewriter, and often they'll give you text containing some typewriter effects that look unprofessional. For one thing, they'll press the Space bar twice after each period that ends a sentence. They'll also use two hyphens (--) instead of a dash (—). Finally, they'll use <u>underline</u> instead of *italics*. Before computerized typesetting, these were necessary compromises because most typewriters cannot adjust letter spacing, make dashes (other than hyphens) or create italics. But you shouldn't let these pre-desktop-publishing remnants degrade the look of your work.

There are two classic dashes (in addition to the hyphen) found in most typefaces: the em dash and the en dash. In whatever typeface at whatever type size, the em dash extends over a space equal to the width of the letter *m* (and the en dash, of the letter *n*) in its particular typeface.

You can use either the long or the short dash in your effort to eliminate double hyphens, but the long dash can leave "holes" in your body text which are unattractive to many people. Also, it is common practice to surround the short dash by spaces but leave the long dash butted up against the text it separates.

Solution: First, don't use the Courier (monospaced) typeface (the "typewriter" typeface) that sets each character in the same amount of space. With Courier, your pages will look exactly as if they were cranked out in the basement of the recreation hall at summer camp. Second, if people give you text containing two spaces between sentences, double hyphens or underlining, use WP's search and replace to get rid of them. Here's how:

Change the typeface to Dutch Roman or any typeface other than Courier. (Position the cursor at the start of the text, press Ctrl-F8 and select your typeface.) Then Alt+F2 will bring up the Replace menu. Search for period-space-space (press period, Space bar, Space bar). Replace with period, Space bar. Then press F2 and WordPerfect will replace each period-two spaces with period-one space.

Second, you can access special characters (such as a true dash) in WP by selecting Typographic Symbols from the WP character set list. Press Ctrl+W to bring up the list. Then with a mouse choose Typographic Symbols as the character set, and double-click on the dash. If you don't use a mouse, press Ctrl+W, Tab, S, T, C, then use the arrow keys to move to the dash.

Now, to replace double hyphens with em dashes and replace underline with italics, you use search and replace, but press Ctrl+W when you get to the Replace With: entry box and make your choices. (You cannot enter these special characters shown in this box from the keyboard [where they do not exist] or as codes.)

To replace all double hyphens with em dashes: Alt+F2, then enter -- (the hyphens), then Tab to move into the Replace With: box. Then press Ctrl+W to access the special character window. Now Tab, 2, T (to select Typographic Symbols), then 3 to move into the character box. Now use the arrow

Choose anything but Courier.

keys to move down three lines and over to the third character, the longer dash. Press Enter, then F2 to complete the re-
placement. Use this technique to search and replace any bullets, dingbats or other special symbols. *Note:* this lengthy
process can be combined with removing double spacing after
periods into a single macro. We'll show you how in Chapter
6. The typewriter-to-typeset conversion macro, called "Typeset," is also included on the companion disk to this book.

Problem: Another holdover from typewriters is using inch
marks (") for quotation marks ("). Within body text, inch
marks can, in fact, be less distracting than true directional
(open and closed) double quotation marks. However, for
pull-quotes and headlines, always take the time to insert true
quotation marks. In a larger, bolder typeface, inch marks look
crude. And true quote marks look better in body text, too, if
the publication is a more formal document such as a catalog
of elegant antiques.

Solution: Replace the inch marks by hand. Press Ctrl+W to
bring up the character set list, then with a mouse choose
Typographic Symbols as the character set and double-click
on the open or close quotation marks as necessary. If you
don't use a mouse, press Ctrl+W, Tab, S, T, C, then use the
arrow keys to move to the quotation marks. This process will
be tedious if you have to do it throughout a lengthy document, but at least fix any inch marks in headlines.

Problem: Yet another holdover from typewriting is the five-
space indent at the start of a paragraph. This standard
typewritter indent is too large for a good typeset look.

Solution: Many publications look better if you eliminate
paragraph indents and instead use extra space to separate
paragraphs, particularly if your text is fully justified with a
straight right margin.

Before you desktop
publish a piece of work, take
a break. Then print it out and
look at it as if you were seeing
it for the first time.
Then, when you've
cleaned up the small problems,
ask the big questions: Does
the design make you want to
read it? Is it spacious enough
and inviting to the intended
audience?

Before you desktop publish
a piece of work, take a break.
Then print it out and look at it
as if you were seeing it for the
first time.
Then, when you've cleaned
up the small problems, ask the
the big questions: Does the
design make you want to read
it? Is it spacious enough and
inviting to the intended
audience?

Figure 5-8: Use narrow indentation particularly with columns.

If you do want to indent paragraphs set in columns, make the indentations shallower. The rule of thumb is, the narrower the column, the less the paragraph indent should be. You can remove extra indentation with WP's search and replace tool in the Edit menu, but you need to know whether the typist inserted one tab or five Space bar spaces.

To replace formatting codes quickly, press Alt+F3 to reveal codes and see if there is a [TAB] or [INDENT] code at the start of every paragraph. If so, press Alt+F2 to bring up the Replace menu. Search for "CODES" of [TAB] (F5) and leave the Replace option blank. Then press F2 to remove all the tabs. If the typist used five spaces instead of a tab, search for five Space bar spaces. To specify what size indent you want for each paragraph, press Shift+F8, 2, 7, and enter the amount (in tenths of an inch) you want the first line of each paragraph to be indented. Then press Enter three times to return to your document. You can experiment with different increments till you get the amount you want.

Search for paragraph tabs and replace them.

FADS & FASHIONS

Problem: People can distinguish quadrillions of different aromas and are also extremely sensitive to variations in loudness of a sound. Likewise, part of the human brain immediately extracts patterns from a visual stimulation and, like it or not, your desktop publication design is ultimately a good or a bad visual stimulation.

Currently there is a fashion, thought to have originated in Seattle, called *grunge*. Part Annie Hall (many layers of contrasting patterns, loose-fitting), part second-hand rose (dusty colors, loud, out-of-date prints), part lumberjack (flannel, plaids, earth tones). The people who've espoused this style of dress may *be* clean, but they don't quite *look* clean. This trend has spread from clothing and popular music to page layout, typeface design and advertising.

Grunge in typefaces leads to almost unreadable letters—some with and some without serifs and each letter a different size from the others in the font. Grunge in page design results in crowded, overlapping zones, eccentric placement of heads and body text, and such. In other words, grunge, like earlier revolts against classical formality (the swirling storms of art nouveau, or the colorful psychedelic style of the late 1960s, for instance) derives its originality and popularity from violating current conventions and standards of taste.

Solution: Although breaking the rules can lead to excellent, even powerful, design, it is unlikely that most of your desktop publishing jobs would benefit from such deliberate provocation of the reader. It is especially unlikely that your boss or customer would respond well to grunge's graffiti-like, sketchy typefaces thrown haphazardly across a page.

Problem: There are several ways to disconcert and annoy people visually. One of them is a page with random, uneven spacing. Some examples: subheads unevenly spaced between sections of text; columns of uneven length and/or width; inconsistent page margins; captions that extend beyond the photos they describe; text shaped to fit into a circle or other geometric shape.

The effects of grunge, the latest fad in design.

Breaking the rules can lead to a great design—or a disaster.

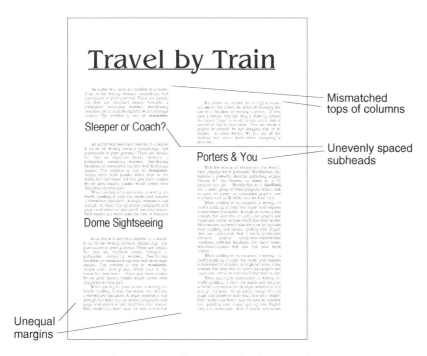

Figure 5-9: Avoid uneven columns and other random spacing.

As you may know, there's a category of creativity called *torture art*—inspiration gone wrong. The usual examples are efforts to make a sculpture out of something inappropriate—building an Eiffel Tower out of toothpicks or hair or something. These efforts usually end up in "believe it or not" museums, which is where they belong. One lesson to be learned from torture art: there is no necessary relationship between *effort* and *result*. If the original idea is daft, the result will be daft too, no matter how hard it was to accomplish.

The fact that WP *allows* you to type a paragraph in the shape of a pyramid doesn't mean you *should*. That would be like "creative" torturing of food—molding chopped ham into the shape of a fish. Serve that and most people are puzzled rather than pleased.

Solution: Take a close look at your margins around the edge of the page and between columns. Adjust unequal margins that should match each other. Look at captions—make sure

Creativity gone wrong leads to "torture art."

the caption doesn't extend beyond the width of the photo it describes. Be sure subheads are consistently spaced throughout the sections, fairly tight against the text that follows.

BAD WHITE

Problem: Sometimes white space can look bad. If you've surrounded a white area with text or a graphic, you've *trapped* some white space. This white space serves no purpose and makes your page look blotchy. (See Figure 5-10.) Usually this happens because you don't have enough text to fill the space, so you've separated the subheads from the text they belong to. Or you have to leave too much space between sections.

Pools or rivers of white space are unattractive.

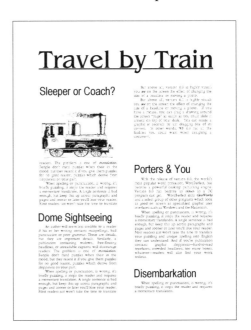

Figure 5-10: There's too much white space between the subhead and the picture. There's also an awkward gap above the first subhead in the right-hand column.

Solution: Enlarge a graphic or use a large type size for a headline. You can also add new text or pull in some existing text from the following page. You could insert a pull-quote (a brief quotation from the text) set in larger type between horizontal rules. Any of these approaches can eliminate the trapped white space.

Problem: A related problem is "rivers." We discussed earlier how justification can create "rivers of white" if a column is too narrow to support justification. WP makes the words on the right side of a column line up by adding space between words. If there is too much of this fill-in space, it can form vertical white patterns within the text blocks.

Solution: Don't use full justification for narrow columns. Or you can make your columns wider. If you must justify a narrow column, make sure that hyphenation is turned on (Shift+F8, 1, 6). And reduce WP's default word space limits from 400 percent to 100 percent (Shift + F8, 7, 9, 1).

THE 8½ X 11 SQUEEZE

Problem: If your publication will be printed on standard letter-size paper, you'll often find this width too narrow for a three-column layout yet too wide for a one-column layout. With a single column, lines stretching all the way across the page are tiring to read unless you double-space or use some other tactic. Most people find it easier to locate the start of each new line if it's not too far from the end of the previous line.

With 8 ½ x 11-inch paper, the best compromise is two columns, but many official publications don't look good when broken into two small columns of text. Classic columns suggest newsletters rather than corporate annual reports or financial plans.

Solution: Create two columns. Make the outside column the narrower one (perhaps one-third the width of the other column), and place the subheads in it. Set the text in the wider column. This arrangement is popular with desktop publishers because it solves the readability problem and also opens up the publication with considerable white space. Yet everything can fit well into the 8 ½-inch limit.

Two unequal columns fit nicely on the standard-size paper used for most desktop-published documents.

For a complete description of how to set up uneven columns in WP, how to import or type text into them, and how to maneuver the cursor around within them, see Chapter 4 under the subhead "Margins & Gutters."

Problem: How to insert a Graphics Box within or across column boundaries (as shown in Figure 5-11).

Solution:

1. Move your cursor to the vertical location where you want the box inserted.

2. Press Alt+F9, 1, 1 to create a new box.

3. Choose Filename, and also enter the file name of your picture.

4. To cause a box to violate the column borders, change the Attach To Paragraph option to Attach To Page. Now you can precisely describe the location on the page where the box will appear.

Special Note on Shadows: In Chapter 2 we discussed how shadows are rarely 100 percent black because that would require a single, strong light source in an otherwise dark room. Unless other design considerations (such as page balance) intervene, you should select less than 100 percent black when you add a shadow to a figure box. Fifty percent or lower is a realistic choice (Alt+F9, 1, 1, 6, 5, 1, 5, then select the shadow color: 2, 2, and type in the percent of black you want).

But you can make shadows even more realistic with a little effort. Not only are most shadows gray rather than black, but they are also blurred at the edges. In CorelDRAW or another drawing/retouching program, load in an image and add a shadow about 50 percent black. Then outline the edge of the shadow (one edge at a time) and use the Edit/Filter/Motion Blur feature to blend the shadow into the white background of the page (see Figure 5-11). You can also use the smear tool to round the corners of the shadow. Then save the file to disk and import it into a borderless WP Figure Box.

Use Attach To Page if you want your box to span column boundaries.

Figure 5-11: To make your shadows highly realistic, smear or airbrush all around the edges.

Figure 5-12: Compare the realism of the 100 percent black shadow on the left to the much lighter shadow on the right, with its blurred edges and rounded corners.

CROWDING

Problem: You've seen people at all-you-can-eat restaurants who don't seem to realize they can go back later. They fill their plates, then start a second layer, piling different foods into a mound. Unappetizing.

In fashion and design, layering rarely results in the grunge or Annie Hall look (to succeed, layering takes considerable care and taste). Instead, too much *stuff* in a page layout usually looks either gorged or accidental, as if things had crashed onto the page.

Somebody might want to save paper and printing costs, and suggest that because your last page is only half-full of text, why not make room for it in the earlier pages, eliminating the last page. Perhaps a writer can't cut *a single precious word* of his or her long article. Perhaps you're doing an ad and you're asked to include extensive descriptions of the product along with five customer testimonials. And they want it all in a 6- x 4-inch space.

Or maybe you've become so mesmerized with clip art, typefaces, boxes, reverses and other design elements that you're trying to put too many things into a single publication. Remember the old saying, "There's no magic unless you do one trick at a time."

Publications get crowded for various reasons.

Lace and doilies have gone the way of the horse-drawn carriage.

Figure 5-13: Elaborate, lacy borders appealed to our great-grandparents.

A hundred years ago, crowding wasn't a problem. It was the style. You've seen pictures of 19th century parlors—crammed with horsehair-stuffed furniture, dripping with doilies, figurines and vases on every level surface, walls jam-packed with paintings. Publications followed this style. For the feel of a doily, designers placed complex border designs around nearly every ad. For the room-full-of-furniture effect, ads often displayed *every item* the store had for sale.

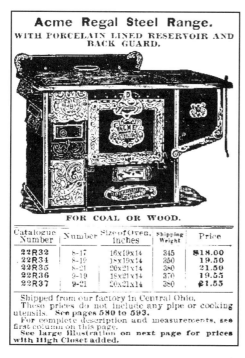

Figure 5-14: 100 years ago they didn't waste any space.

Gone are the gewgaws and gargoyles.

In this century, instead of the flourishes and frills so beloved by our great-grandparents, the trend—particularly in architecture and advertising—has been toward vast, clean spaces with no borders, often no pictures and few words. The illustration in Figure 5-15 takes this style to the extreme, with its almost stark simplicity. But you should keep in mind the maxim *less is more*; that's the essence of 20th century style in architecture, clothing, publication design and practically everything else visual.

Figure 5-15: Today's minimalist style often endeavors to create a *mood*, instead of providing many specific details.

Solution: Subtraction—the magic of Delete and Undo. Many artists appreciate the computer simply because, aside from everything else it does, a computer allows you to quickly and painlessly add or subtract words and pictures.

Some designers start by putting *lots of things* on the page, then take them out one by one until the design looks clean and pleasing to the eye.

Figure 5-16: Random in the worst ways, this party invitation says: *talent and taste weren't involved in this.*

This invitation looks uncoordinated, erratic, spastic, as if the designer mindlessly threw in anything that happened to be available, placing things without regard to balance. It's not *deliberately* messy (a style that can work). Instead, it's just randomly messy and thoroughly ugly.

How will we deal with this *accident*, this pouring of information into Figure 5-16? Sure, it's a party invitation, so we want the piece to look upbeat and informal. But we can create that mood without creating a mess.

Try first to free up some white space: take out some text, a sidebar, graphic elements or whatever to give your document an open, inviting look and help you avoid this collision of disorganized text and graphics.

To fix this piece, we relegated all the text to small type at the bottom of the page. Then we used CorelDRAW to reverse the flower stem. If you have a strong line like this stem, you want it to guide the eye *into* your message; not out and away from the page, as in Figure 5-16. We superimposed the clock face on the flower, gaining a much-needed area of white space, and, finally, expanded the word *Party*.

Free up some white space to fix a crowded design.

Once again this year we're having our
"Welcome Spring" Party!
We hope you can come and enjoy the
warm weather with us. Swimming in the pool!
8 PM Friday at Denise Johnson's

Figure 5-17: A distinct improvement. No clutter, just the essentials and lots of space.

Figure 5-18 shows another approach to achieve a simple but effective design. It's also a good example to study for balance. The characters of the Optima Bold typeface we used in the illustration complement the strong, dominant tree graphic. Or you could pick a typeface that *looks treelike*, with skinny strokes and a tall, thin quality, maybe italic.

BALANCE

Problem: But how do you know where to place the elements to get a balanced composition?

Solution: Move the text block and the graphic around, to find an arrangement that looks at rest on the page—not too high, too low, or too far to the left or right. The computer lets you resize, cut and move pieces around with great ease.

Some people find it useful to imagine a page they're designing as a square white ceramic plate resting precariously on a marble. Then imagine that the pieces of graphic and text are made of metal—that they have weight. Move them all around on the page until the white plate doesn't tip in any direction. It's balanced. Now turn the page a quarter-turn. Is it still balanced? Then turn it upside down and look again. These maneuvers might seem silly at first, but they work.

Objects like trees and houses need an anchor: In Figure 5-18, we added a moon in the upper right corner to finish balancing this page (cover the moon with your hand and see how that throws things too much to the lower left). Finally, we added a line at the bottom to anchor the tree. Things that have their roots or foundations in the earth, such as trees, bridges, buildings, etc., usually don't look good floating in white—they seem to need an anchor line.

Check for balance by imagining a plate on top of a marble.

Figure 5-18: Simple and open, this version has a beautiful, almost Oriental elegance.

A perfectly symmetrical thing is, of course, always in balance—its components are equally distant from the four sides of the page, and equidistant from each other. So they are in perfect balance, but they are also usually *boring*. In cooking, the only truly *safe* ingredient is water—it has no flavor so it merely dilutes whatever you add it to. Similarly, too much symmetry can reduce your page design to blandness. You want to learn the tricks of placing things so they result in both variety and balance. You don't want to put in too much of anything, causing that item to dominate and overshadow the other elements. On the other hand, you can't play it too safe and make everything equal.

How can you check for balance? Print a copy of your page, tape it to the wall, and squint. Squinting reduces the black/white contrast and blends the text elements into gray masses that you can compare with the graphic elements *as shapes*. Your goal is to arrange these elements so that the page looks balanced even when you turn it upside down or sideways.

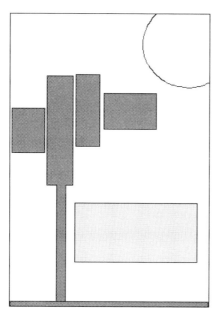

Figure 5-19: Try to look at your page as if it contained blocks of grays and lines. Does anything throw the page out of balance? Is there too much on the left side?

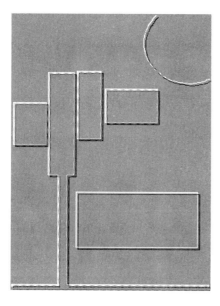

Figure 5-20: Also look at the *lines* (ignoring for the moment the balance). Are they spaced so that one area of the page doesn't dominate?

Cover a sample
page with a sheet
of blank paper.

Another trick is to cover part of your page with a piece of blank white paper. First print a *proof,* a sample of your work. Then slide a piece of white paper halfway onto your printed page. Then slide it onto the other half so you can see how many lines are on the left half versus the right half. Do this again, but compare the top half versus the bottom half. Then repeat the process, but this time look for imbalance between the black and the white content (not the lines).

In Figure 5-18, the moon has particular weight because it is a circle surrounded by what are essentially rectangles of space. The odd thing out has a little more weight.

CONTRAST

Problem: Your pages are boring, things are too much the same. You've used only one typeface, or you have no graphics, or your top margin is the same size as all the others. Figure 5-21 shows a page with unrelieved gray sameness.

Figure 5-21: Few people like to read gray pages.

Figure 5-22: Adding graphics is one way to create contrast.

Solution: In Figure 5-22, we drop a frog into the middle of the text. Which of the two publications do you think most people would be more likely to read?

Another good way to liven up a dull mass of text is to break it into sections, adding subheads, rules, symbols or other items that stand out from the text. Or add pull-quotes set in larger type bordered above and below by two thick rules. A pull-quote is a particularly intriguing sentence or two from the text that invites the reader to look into the subject further.

Contrast can also be achieved by putting something plain next to something beautiful. You know the trick: Marilyn Monroe had her black dot, her mole. That flaw in the otherwise lovely face merely made the beauty more potent. It's what vinegar does to sugar. A couple of years ago, a drop-dead beautiful actress brought her average-looking sister with her to the Academy Awards. They were all smiles, but one of the smiles was decidedly more radiant by contrast with the other.

If all else fails, add a frog.

Figure 5-23: Marilyn's imperfection, her mole, amplified her beauty.

REPETITION

Problem: You don't want to bore people with pages that lack contrast. However, you do want your document to be consistent and coherent. These goals pull the designer in two directions at once. If you don't want to bore people with zero contrast, how do you create order and consistency?

It's another kind of balance: variety within repetition.

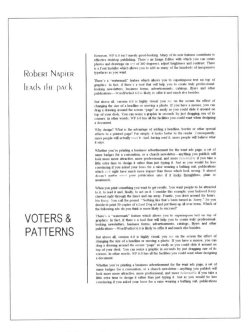

Figure 5-24: The two subheads don't match.

Solution: Your work will look cleaner if you select a single typeface and type size for all similar subheads.

Figure 5-24 contains two subheads in the margin. Both are doing the same job, so they should be graphically and typographically equivalent. However, the upper one is a script-like boldface in initial capitals and lowercase. The lower subhead is sans-serif, not bold, all-caps. We fixed this discontinuity in Figure 5-25.

Figure 5-25: The page holds together better when the same typeface is used for all subheads.

If you use icons, bullets or dingbats, choose a small set and use only a few—don't just mix and match at random.

✔ A bulleted list should have the *same* bullet style at the start of each item. The same applies to icons, symbols and dingbats. If you want to use a few different symbols (a telephone for phone numbers, a scissors for coupons, etc.), be sure they have a family resemblance. Don't mix, for instance, silhouettes with line drawings.

✔ People find it comforting when graphic and font elements are repeated. That's the theory behind matching accessories in fashion—the handkerchief in the pocket matches or complements the tie and holds things together visually.

There are other ways to achieve repetition and consistency. For an advertisement, the Shear Perfection hair salon asked us to do "something Cocteau-like," as they put it. We got lucky and came up with a drawing that they ended up using as their logo as well.

Drawings like this one shown in Figure 5-26 seem to be the result of absent-minded doodling. In fact, unless you're like Picasso or Hockney or somebody terribly gifted with a pen, you might spend an hour (as we did) getting these few lines just right. There was much redrawing, moving the pieces around onscreen into different positions, adding hair, subtracting hair, etc. Nonetheless, the computer can make this an hour-long, rather than a day-long, job.

Figure 5-26: Notice how the lettering repeats the line style in the drawing.

You can repeat the style of a graphic by selecting a similar typeface.

For this ad we wanted the typeface to repeat the shape of the lines in the hair. We had a font called *Palette*, which has the same pen-stroke quality. The shape of a pen's nib differs from one model to another—some are flat, some round. Flat nibs create thick to thin areas around curves, and most drawing programs let you select a simulated nib shape. Likewise, there's usually a thinning of the line where the pen hits or leaves the paper. The strokes of Palette imitated a flat-nib pen, the tool we used to draw the face.

There were several other things we did to add to the *feel* of this piece. We looked at the page and played around with different shapes and sizes using CorelPHOTO-PAINT to distort and adjust the various objects on the page.

To add variety, imitate a line shape but slant it backward.

Our plan was to make things look disarrayed—a little wrong—without being obvious about it. The operational words were *split ends* and *flyaway*.

First we stretched the letter spacing in the words BAD HAIR but not in the word DAY. That's a bit disconcerting. The text has come loose, isn't conforming to size expectations. Then we sized the text to match the line thickness in the drawing.

We noticed that in this typeface the capital letter I in HAIR looked too much like the D. It wasn't very readable. So by hand we drew an I that would repeat the shape of several lines in the drawing but violate the rightward slant of the rest of the letters (and of normal handwriting).

The question mark seemed too small, so we enlarged it and moved it up, creating another hair-shape repetition—and also creating something else that is just a little out of place.

Finally, we copied the dot below the question mark and used it as the dot over the I to repeat small shapes (the nose, the I's dot, and the dot below the question mark). Cover the dot over the I with your finger and see if you think that subtracts from the unity of the design. Repetition, as any musician or painter can tell you, creates cohesion—but one of the best tricks is to slightly vary the repeated elements.

The look of this ad should subtly reinforce the text message, *bad hair day*. The key word is *subtly*. So ask yourself, what *is* bad hair? Maybe make a list of the qualities you're expressing: it's frizzy, not neat—strands of hair have gotten away from the overall pattern. We don't want our ad to look haphazard, but with these several little adjustments, we can preserve the unity of the design while conveying the idea of something slowly coming apart at the split ends.

Of course, if you were playing around with this page, you could achieve the same sense of looseness in many other ways. These are the steps we took, but there are lots of things you could do to make the reader *feel* the message in addition to merely reading it.

Make your pages *look* like what they say—make form support content.

APPROPRIATENESS

Problem: Even the best-designed piece can fail if the style works against the content. You don't testify in court in the outfit you'd wear to a beach party.

Solution: Be sure the typefaces and graphics work with, not against, the goals of the publication. The cover of the travel brochure in Figure 5-27 is well balanced. It successfully combines repetition with variety. In general it's a solid enough design, as a *design*. But the look isn't right somehow.

Somehow it doesn't say "travel," "relax," "fun." Also, there's something jarring about the typeface used for the word Zanzibar. And what does that silhouette of an Edwardian bedroom have to do with exotic Zanzibar? The graphic in this piece says *relax*, so that's good. But it doesn't say *have fun*. And it also says *at home*. We're trying to say *leave home*. We need a different image.

Figure 5-27: Although nicely proportioned and otherwise clean-looking, this brochure doesn't look like travel.

First we get rid of the block of justified text. (You can always put the details inside the brochure, not on the cover.) Who can relax with all that to read? This isn't a homework assignment, it's a lure.

Figure 5-28: We're inviting them on a cruise, and this really looks inviting. (Clip Art courtesy of CorelDRAW!)

Then we replace the hair-brushing scene with a soaring bird, and change the typeface to something Oriental and foreign-looking for the word Zanzibar. We also reinforce the exotic motif by surrounding the word with a border reminiscent of an Oriental rug.

MOVING ON

Word Perfect 6.0 includes a number of features that make life easier for the desktop publisher. In the next chapter we'll focus on how WordPerfect's "styles" can give your publications consistency and preserve your successful designs for reuse in other desktop publishing jobs. Macros automate even the most menu-driven WP feature. For example, we'll see how to adjust letter spacing by simply pressing two keys (instead of going through seven nested menus). And specialized "keyboards" and "button bars" allow you to make macros themselves more automatic. You can do most anything in WP with a keypress or the click of a mouse.

We'll explore these various tools next and, using specific examples, show how to make your desktop publishing projects easier and more effective.

6 Shortcut Tools

Some of WordPerfect 6.0's most powerful features are its shortcut tools—styles, macros, keyboards and button bars. Sometimes you'll have to go through a series of complex maneuvers to accomplish something in WP. You'll move through several submenus, spending a good deal of time remembering which keys access the correct initial menu, reading options in the menus, pressing function keys and making selections. Styles, macros, keyboards and button bars can eliminate these repetitive tasks.

About Macros

Put repetitive tasks into macros and styles.

A typical example of a repetitive task is kerning a headline—moving two letters slightly closer together to make the headline look better. If you do this manually, you must press Shift+F8, 7, 6, 1, type in .01, and press Enter, Enter, Enter, Enter every time you make a slight adjustment. Now you've moved the letter that's to the right of your cursor $1/100$ of an inch closer to the letter to the left of your cursor. You'll likely go through this process several times just to get one letter pair spaced exactly as you want it. How tedious to have to repeat that entire key sequence each time.

Further, let's assume that you have to do this task several times a day. A macro is the solution. You can have WP *record* your series of keyboard actions, then give the recording a name and it becomes a macro. Forever after you can just invoke the macro's name instead of going through the complicated steps to accomplish the goal. In effect, a macro becomes a new command, a new feature in WP. It's a custom feature you've added to WP's set of tools.

About Keyboards & Buttons

Beyond that, you can add macros (or other WP commands) to sets of specialized "keyboards." Then you don't even have to remember the macro's name or press Alt+F10 to invoke it.

Say that you've created a macro that reduces type size. This way you can quickly see how a given headline looks when made smaller. However, you don't want to have to go through a set of menus (Alt+F10, then select the macro you've named "Reduce") each time. After all, macros are supposed to help you avoid all that menu-surfing.

You can create a *keyboard*, a special set of key assignments. Then, to reduce a headline, all you have to do is press Alt+R or Ctrl+R or whatever key combination you assigned to that macro. The macro runs, and the menus and commands are automatically carried out—while you sit back and watch. It will probably be done too fast for you to really see the action, but you get the idea.

Yet another way to invoke macros is to assign them to a *button bar*. Assigning WP commands, WP features, menu items or personal macros to button bars is simple. For mouse users, a button bar can be a most efficient tool. Not only can you see the text names of all the items on the bar, you can also see icons to remind you of the purpose of the button.

Do you "wear more than one hat"—one day sending out correspondence, another day designing a desktop publishing document? If so, you can have *sets* of specialized button bars, style libraries, keyboards and macros. Use the "normal writing" sets when typing correspondence. Use the "DTP" sets when doing page layout.

We'll explore all these tools in this chapter. Styles, macros, keyboards and button bars aren't specifically designed for desktop publishing alone. Yet in some ways, these four shortcut tools are among the most important features that WP provides. Practically anything WP can do can be made more

Put related macros into specialized keyboards and button bars.

efficient and easier to remember via these techniques. The styles tool is the most directly useful tool for desktop publishing, so we'll spend most of our time describing styles. However, we will go into the other three tools in sufficient depth for you to use them, too, in your DTP work.

STYLES

WP's "styles" are close cousins to macros. However, a style can be more versatile than a macro in certain special cases. If you insert *style codes* throughout a document, you can then make document-wide changes simply by changing the style. You won't have to change each *instance* of that style within the document. Furthermore, if you've used the style in several documents, each one will automatically conform to the change you made.

Use styles to format large projects which may need revision.

Macros are extremely useful, but styles are best for formatting large documents that you might need to change or reuse in the future. In other words, if a document will be a *template* for future documents (such as a quarterly report), format it with styles. If you use macros for this task, you will have to change each formatting code in each place it was used in a document. A macro inserts normal formatting codes just as if you were pressing the appropriate function key or key combination (for example, F6 for boldface). It simply automates the insertion process. Let's look at an example.

EXAMPLE OF A STYLE

Assume that you have been asked to produce your company's quarterly report. This is a highly formal, 10-page document—read by everyone from the chairman to agitated stockholders. This kind of job is similar to a term paper in that you need to provide footnotes and even a bibliography. Footnotes and bibliographic entries are tedious to construct, requiring "hung" (or hanging) paragraphs. The format for these reference items is the reverse of the normal paragraph format—the first line starts at the margin and the rest of the lines are indented (see Figure 6-1).

The company has decided to acquire three new divisions this year as a result of gross revenue increases and the surplus capital availability.* We will engineer this through our sister division in Seattle and also work with a consulting firm

* Capital availability is a result of our having huge writeoffs in 1993 due to our summary change in bookeeping and the total elimination and retroactive shut - down of R&D plans. This has made cash.

Figure 6-1: A hung paragraph requires special codes you can combine to make a "style."

DO IT WITH STYLES

In WordPerfect 6.0, there are three ways to accomplish things like this special format. One is to start each entry with F4, Shift+Tab, which inserts the codes [Lft Indent][Back Tab] into your text. Another is to create a macro that will do it for you each time (see the "Macros" section later in this chapter). But the best way, particularly if you're going to be doing it over and over, is with a style.

HUNG PARAGRAPHS

The following paragraph is an example of the style we've named "Hung."

In this style format, the paragraphs don't start with a
   first-line indent, and the rest of the lines start flush
   to the left margin. A hung paragraph has all lines
   indented *except* the first one.

This way of formatting paragraphs is most commonly used in bibliographic or footnote entries. However, it can also be used to highlight the first line of an article, setting it off from the rest of the text. Hung paragraphs can also be used to insert large initial caps (drop or raised caps). (The initial letter of the first word of each paragraph is greatly enlarged.)

To turn off this style (it will remain in effect until you do turn it off), you can just delete the style code. In other words, because Hung is a "Paragraph" style, the code reappears at the start of each new paragraph as you write. So, by deleting this code (pressing Alt+F3 to reveal the codes, then cursoring over to the [Para Style: Hung] code and pressing Delete), you escape its influence and turn it off.

You can see this happen by starting a style code then pressing the reveal codes key (Alt+F3). Type a few words and press Return. You will see the style code reappear after the Return. To remove the style for this new paragraph, backspace to delete the code. (You don't have to reveal the codes in order to turn things off; it just shows you what's happening.) However, WP allows you to automatically turn off a style so you don't have to delete the codes. To see your options for turning a style off, select Enter Key Action in the Edit Style Menu (press Alt+F8, highlight a style, then press 6 and then 3). For more on this technique, see "Styles" in the WordPerfect 6.0 *User's Guide*.

Delete a style code to escape its effects.

THREE KINDS OF STYLES

Before we create our Hung style, let's explain the zone of influence that styles can have: they can be applied to paragraphs, characters or entire documents. Once you press En-

Styles have three ranges of influence in a document.

ter, starting a new paragraph, you'll escape a style if it's been defined as a *character* style. (You can also escape *paragraph* styles this way, provided that your style's Enter Key Action is set to option 2, Turn Style Off.)

Paragraph Styles

A paragraph style affects an entire paragraph and is useful for establishing a typeface, type size, position on the page, etc., or for headlines and subheads. A paragraph style carries over from one paragraph to the next unless you remove it by deleting the style code that appears at the beginning of each paragraph. (The paragraph style code reappears at the beginning of each new paragraph unless you intervene.)

Character Styles

Character styles affect all the text from the position where you insert the style (the cursor position) forward to the end of the paragraph.

Open Styles

An open style affects the entire document from the point where you insert the style to the end of the document.

HOW TO CREATE A STYLE

We want to create a style called *Hung* and make its effects paragraph-wide, so we'll choose Paragraph Style. To create a style and save it to the disk for future use:

1. Press Alt+F8, 2.
2. Name it "Hung."
3. Press Enter, Enter.
4. Press the same keys you would use if you were creating a hung paragraph: F4, Shift+Tab. You'll see the codes appear in the editing box.
5. Exit the editing mode with F7.
6. Press Enter to save the style to disk, naming it *Hung*.

Now, whenever you call up the Styles menu (Alt+F8), you can load your style in from disk by pressing 8 (Retrieve) and typing *Hung*. You'll see your Hung style waiting for you to apply to a paragraph. (To avoid the last retrieving step, you can create a "styles library." We'll explain later.)

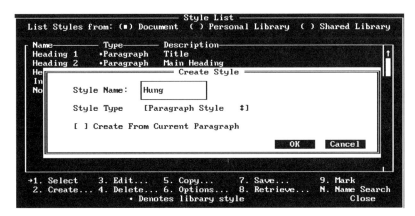

Figure 6-2: Creating a style.

SNATCHING A STYLE

Another way to create a style is to just move your cursor to a paragraph that is already formatted the way you want it, copy the style, and save it to disk. You press Alt+F8, 2, then select "Create From Current Paragraph." This approach is often easier than repeating the keystrokes.

ADDING A STYLE TO AN EXISTING DOCUMENT

To add a style to an existing document, block the text you want to apply the style to (using Alt+F4, or the F12 function key on some keyboards, and the arrow keys). You can block an entire document if you wish by pressing Home, Home, Down arrow, then Alt+F4, Home, Home, Up arrow.

Inserting a Style

To insert a style, press Alt+F8 to call up the styles library and cursor down until the style you want is highlighted. Then press Enter. The style-on (and -off, if applicable) codes will be inserted. This is just like the way you would add italics or other formatting codes to previously written text. If you look at the codes, however (by pressing Alt+F3), you'll find that instead of [Lft Indent][Back Tab] (the usual specific codes to create our hung paragraph), you'll see [Para Style: Hung].

CHANGING A STYLE

Now assume that your boss returned your quarterly report and its extensive bibliography with the comment: "The report is unsatisfactory. Remember, the chairman wants footnotes to extend into the margins of our reports! Please resubmit the report in the correct format."

Variations of this unhappy message, of course, come from many sources—copy editors, typesetters, committees, art directors—even from you if you should decide that a particular format looks wrong in a document.

Styles really come into their own and prove their worth in unfortunate situations like this. Because they are contained in a library—and thus separate from the documents they govern—styles are easily changed. Imagine the problems you'd face if your quarterly report was 50 pages long and you had to remove all the original codes embedded within the document by hand and replace them with new ones by hand. Even if you created a macro to automate this process, you'd still be in for unnecessary extra work because macros just automate (mimic) direct entry. You would still have to change each code individually.

If you've used the Hung style, your 50-page report isn't filled with [Lft Indent][Back Tab] codes that create all the hung paragraphs. Instead, it's filled with [Para Style: Hung] codes. So the solution is simple: You just redefine what *Hung* means to WP. Since WP looks up this style in the styles library

Styles are lifesavers when you need to revise the format of a large document.

each time it appears when your document is printing, all you need to do is change the one code in the Hung style, and every reference to that style in any document will automatically change when that document is printed.

Styles Are Filters

Styles, then, are filters through which documents go on their way to the printer. Unlike embedded codes, a simple change to a style in your styles library can have a global effect on any document containing the codes for that style.

So you can merely edit the style we've called Hung to make the hung paragraphs extend into the margin. Just remove [Lft Indent] from the Hung style and the entire document will be automatically reformatted the way the boss wants it.

```
           This is an example of a hung paragraph which is aligned with the
               left margin.
       This is an example of a hung paragraph which moves outside the left
           margin.
```
```
[Lft Indent][Back Tab]This is an example of a hung paragraph which is aligned with the[SRt]
left margin.[HRt]
[HRt]
[Back Tab]This is an example of a hung paragraph which moves outside the left[SRt]
margin.
```

Figure 6-3: The boss wants the paragraphs to start in the left margin, like the second paragraph in this figure.

Changing Hung

To edit this style, press Alt+F8. If Hung isn't already in your list of styles, bring it into the Style Editor by pressing 8 (Retrieve) and typing *Hung*. Now move an arrow key to highlight Hung, then press 3 (Edit), and you'll see the codes which define the Hung style: [Lft Indent][Back Tab].

Now press 4 to move into the editing box, and use the Delete key to remove the [Lft Indent] code. Then press F7 to exit the editing box and press Enter, Enter to get rid of the Styles menu. That's all there is to changing the formatting of the *entire* report.

CREATING A STYLES LIBRARY

Let's assume that you've created several other styles for quarterly reports—typefaces and type sizes, subheads, position of page numbers and other formatting specifications.

Because you're going to have to do more of these reports in the future, you'll want to save this set of styles in a personal library that you can call up from the disk drive whenever you need it. WP also provides a default library called "Document," which contains any initial codes you defined with Shift+F1 Setup. These are your default preferences for most of the documents you work with. And WP includes another set of optional libraries called "Shared," which are for use on networks.

Storing Your Styles Libraries

Now you want to create a personal library, which we'll call "QRPT," to use when formatting your quarterly reports. If you haven't already told WP where to store your personal libraries, press Shift+F1, 5, 2, 1 and type in "Mystyles" or whatever you want to call it. At this point you can tell WP to store and retrieve personal styles from a particular subdirectory on your disk. If you don't specify a name and location, WP will default to the WP 6.0 directory.

All styles that you've created for the quarterly report—headlines, subheads, margins, hung paragraphs, etc.—will be listed when you press Alt+F8. You now want to save this collection of styles into a style library. Use the arrow keys to move to each style and press the Space bar to select each one. An asterisk (*) will appear next to each selected style. Then

Store sets of related styles in "personal styles libraries."

press 7, SAVE, and type in "QRPT.STY" or whatever you want to call this library. (It's a good idea to add the .STY extension so you'll remember these are styles library files.)

LOADING A STYLES LIBRARY

Three months from now, you'll want to load this set of styles from your disk and use it for the next report. Press Alt+F8, 8, "QRPT.STY," and you'll see that all the styles in the QRPT library are now available for use. One tip: if a document contains many styles, that could slow up WP while you're editing the document. To avoid this problem, you can *assign* rather than *retrieve* a library. Assigning has the same effect as retrieving (it filters the document through the assigned style during printing) but won't slow the editing process (just the *printing* process). To assign: Alt+F8, 6, 1, then type "QRPT.STY" and you've got all your styles.

OTHER USES FOR STYLES

Another use for styles is when you are creating a large document, such as a company newsletter, that will be worked on by many different people. By giving each person working on the newsletter the same library of styles, including headings, subheads, chapter openings, footers and any other page features or formats, you will keep the entire project under control. Since styles are not tied to individual documents, everyone will conform to the same formats—everyone will use *your* styles, not individual formatting codes.

Styles can enforce consistency when several people work on the same project.

Automating Your Styles

Note: If you find yourself using styles often, you might want to create some macros which insert styles automatically (so you don't have to press Alt+F8 and select a style each time). See the "Macros" section of this chapter for more on macros.

OPEN STYLES

Up to now, we've focused on *paired* styles, codes which turn on and then turn off formatting or typefaces for a word, paragraph or other block of text. Italics and boldface are examples of paired codes.

Use open styles to affect an entire document.

Another kind of style, called an *open* style, is intended to be turned on and remain in effect throughout a document. A style for margin settings, for example, would usually be created as an open style so that it would be global to the entire publication. So would a style for justified alignment. You can even make a style out of a piece of standard text, such as "Dear Sir." Using styles in this way, you can start your business letters in a consistent way, with the correct margins, the date, and so forth. However, it is often just as easy to use a macro rather than a style for these purposes.

MACROS

Like all powerful tools, WordPerfect works better for you if you personalize it. Because no two writers or DTP designers approach their tasks the same way, there are provisions in WordPerfect for customizing *the WordPerfect program itself* to suit your individual needs.

A simple example is the Shift+F1 key which reveals a "Setup menu" of choices, various ways you can make the program perform the way you prefer. You can, for example, decide whether or not you want the name of the file you are currently working on to appear in the lower left of the screen, whether you want the program to beep to alert you to special conditions, and other preferences.

AUTOMATING TASKS

Yet for all its ease of use and thoughtful design, the people who wrote WordPerfect could not possibly make it behave the way you would wish in every particular situation. They couldn't include, for example, a way to print your personal name and address whenever you press Alt+A.

However, they have included many remarkable tools that help you personalize the program for the kind of writing and designing you do regularly.

WordPerfect includes a programming language for creating macros. This language has all the fundamental commands found in other computer programming languages, but you don't need to *program* the commands into WP unless you want to. You can *record*—just execute a series of commands while the Record Macro feature is turned on, give a name to the series of commands, and WP will record what you do and save the pattern as a macro. Then you can have WP carry out this task when you simply provide the name of the macro (or even use a simple key combination from a keyboard or click on a button bar icon).

At their most elementary level, macros merely reduce the number of keys or commands required to accomplish a task or a set of tasks. Fully utilized, however, macros can transform the way you use WordPerfect, making it respond to your way of writing, designing and thinking. Just as new shoes are more efficient and pleasant once they adapt themselves to the shapes of your feet and your way of walking, so will your word processor be easier to use and make you more comfortable and productive after you customize it. When you know how to create and modify your own macros, WordPerfect can become a much more effective desktop publishing instrument.

> You don't need to "program" macros; you can record them.

YOUR FIRST MACRO

Nothing could be easier. Let's make a macro that types in your name and address. Then we'll assign it to a keyboard so you can just press Alt+A any time you want WP to type it into a document.

Press Ctrl+F10 and type in *nameaddr*. That will be the name of our macro. Press Enter. Now WP will "watch what you do and learn to imitate it"—open a menu, type in a selection, whatever. So type in your name and address. When you are finished, press Ctrl+F10 again to end the recording sequence.

> Creating your first macro couldn't be easier.

That's it. Let's test it. Press Alt+F10 and type in *nameaddr*. Press Enter and you should see WP slavishly type in what you taught it.

CREATING SHORTCUT KEYS

Nice as it is, our *nameaddr* macro would be even easier to use if we could assign a shortcut key combination to it. Here's how: press Shift+F1, 4. You'll see a list of the current keyboards. [Original] is the one that comes with WP as a default. We'll create one for desktop publishing, so press 2 and type in *DTP*. Then press 1, Alt+A, 5, R. Now we'll add our macro to this keyboard. Type in *nameaddr* and press Enter, F7, 1 (to select DTP as the currently active keyboard), then press Enter to leave the Setup window.

Now you should be back in the normal document editing window. Try pressing Alt+A and watch your name/address macro do its job.

Note: If you are using a custom keyboard like our DTP keyboard, you can always return to the Original WP keyboard by pressing Ctrl+6.

ADDING A MACRO TO A BUTTON BAR

Like keyboards, you can have as many different button bars as you want. If you don't currently have a button bar visible, press Alt+V, B to make one visible. Now, to add our macro to this button bar, press Alt+V, S, E, C, and use the arrow keys to select *nameaddr*. Then press F7 to exit and you should see your macro on the button bar.

SOME USEFUL FACTS ABOUT MACROS

You can specify where WP will store your macros.

WP saves macros in the directory you specified during setup for the Macro/Keyboard/Button Bar files. Macro files are similar to normal WP document files, but they have a .WPM extension on the file name. You can load them into WP and edit them if you wish, changing, for example, your address. You will see various "commands" in WP's macro language. For example, our NAMEADDR.WPM file looks like this:

```
DISPLAY(Off!)
Type("Richard Mansfield")
HardReturn
Type("14 Cannonite Drive")
HardReturn
Type("Roaring Gulch, ND 14522")
HardReturn
```

If you are interested, there are dozens of commands in the WP language that allow you to do many things you cannot do by simply recording keystrokes. For example, you could prevent a macro from carrying out its instructions if the user invoked it while working in some mode other than the normal document-editing screen mode:

```
IF(?EditScreen)
DISPLAY(Off!)
Type("Richard Mansfield")
HardReturn
Type("14 Cannonite Drive")
HardReturn
Type("Roaring Gulch, ND 14522")
HardReturn
ENDIF
```

The WP macro language is similar to the computer language called BASIC. These languages are often quite easy to understand, since many of their commands are common English words. The WP commands listed above say, "If the edit screen is active, then do the following. If not, do nothing."

The Edit Macro feature is a second way to edit macros—and a way to flip between editing and recording so you can see the translation of your actions into commands. Press Home, Ctrl+F10. Then type in the name of the macro you want to edit. Press Enter and you can begin recording. Select things from menus, type in text, whatever. When you want to see the results (WP's translation of your actions into its macro language), press Shift+F3. Then, to record again, press Shift+F3 again. It's an on/off toggle so you can go back and forth at will.

Flip between editing and recording with Edit Macro.

There is much more to macros than we have space for here. If you're interested in doing more with them, select Macros from the WP Help menu.

SOME HELPFUL DTP MACROS

The optional disk that can be ordered to supplement this book includes a set of macros, button bars and keyboards which are specialized for desktop publishing. But here is a selection of macros you can type in and save to disk for later use. After we finish creating these macros, we'll add them (and any others you might want) to a personalized keyboard and button bar.

First we have to know which disk directory holds your Macro/Keyboard/Button Bar files. If you don't recall the name of the directory, press Shift+F1, 5. Now look at #2 and you'll find the directory name.

When creating these macros by copying them from the listings below, type in *exactly* what you see (the typeface, type size, etc., do not matter, but typos *do* matter).

Macro: Kern to the Left

This macro moves a character $1/100$ of an inch to the left. Open a new document (press Alt+F, N). Then type the following into this new document:

```
DISPLAY(Off!)
Advance(ADvanceLeft!;0.01")
```

Then save this document to the directory where your Macro/Keyboard/Button Bar files are kept. Press F10, then type in the name of the directory and the file name *lkern.wpm*. You should type something like this:

```
C:\WPMACS\LKERN.WPM
```

But substitute your directory name for WPMACS. Now you can test the kerning. Type in some text, then put the cursor between two letters. Press Alt+F10 and type in *lkern*. Your macro should move the letters slightly closer together. Do it several times in Page or Graphics View, and watch the results.

After you type in your macro command, test it.

Macro: Kern to the Right

This next macro moves a character $1/100$ of an inch to the right. Open a new document (press Alt+F, N). Then type the following into this new document:

DISPLAY(Off!)
Advance(ADvanceRight!;0.01")

Now save this file the same way as described above, but name it *rkern.wpm*. Now you can freely and very easily kern any headlines that look like they could use it.

Macro: Kern With Letter Spacing

This next method of kerning is less precise than the letter-pair kerning described above. You first block all the text you want to kern (press Alt+F4, then use the arrow keys to select the text), then this macro pulls *all* the blocked letters together, reducing the space between them by 10 percent. However, if you have a lot of text with significant space between the letters, this is a quick way to solve the problem.

As before, open a new document (press Alt+F, N). Then type the following into this new document:

DISPLAY(Off!)
WordLetterSpacing(Optimal!;90)

Now save this file the same way as described above, but name it *kernon.wpm*.

If you *don't* block the text first, using kernon.wpm will reduce letter spacing in *all* text from the cursor position forward. We'll now create a second macro which allows you to move the cursor to a place in the document where you can turn the spacing adjustment off via a second macro:

Open a new document (press Alt+F, N). Then type the following into this new document:

DISPLAY(Off!)
WordLetterSpacing(Optimal!;Optimal!)

Now save this file as *kernoff.wpm*.

Turn letter spacing on and off with two separate macros.

Macro: Rotating

Rotating text isn't the most common activity, but when you need to put a vertical credit line next to a photo, or if you decide that a headline would look good tipped on its side—rotating does the trick. Text rotation is quite time-consuming if you do it manually, and it's hard to remember the necessary menus, but with this macro, you'll be able to rotate in a jiffy.

Open a new document (press Alt+F, N). Then type the following:

```
DISPLAY(Off!)
BoxCreate(FigureBox!)
BoxContentType(Text!)
BoxContentEdit
Input(Type in the text you want to rotate. Press Enter when done.)
BoxTextAngle(Degrees90!)
SubstructureExit
BoxBorderStyle(NoBorder!)
BoxAttachTo(Page!)
BoxWidth(AutoWidth!)
BoxEnd(Save!)
```

Now save this file as *rotate.wpm.*

Since we attached this rotated text to *Page!,* you can freely move it around to wherever you want to place it. It's easiest to click and drag the rotated piece of text with the mouse, but if you don't use a mouse, press Alt+F9, 1, 2, then select the text's box number. Now you'll be in the Graphics Box window. Press 8 to adjust the position of the text.

Macro: Typewriter-to-Typesetter Cleanup

You'll sometimes get disk files other people have written that are to be inserted into your desktop published document. If these people were taught typing on a *typewriter,* they'll probably do some things that will look bad when your document is printed: they'll double-space between sentences, use two hyphens instead of a solid em dash, and underline instead of italicize.

This macro will go through and change double spaces to single spaces, hyphens to dashes, and then bring up a built-in WP macro that allows you to replace any underlining with italics. *Note:* you cannot directly type in this macro because hyphens are a special code that can only be inserted into a macro by *recording* the hyphens. So, you should record these search-and-replace actions. Here's what your finished macro should look like if you load it into the editing view:

```
DISPLAY(Off!)
PosDocTop
SearchString(" ")
ReplaceString(" ")
ReplaceForward()
PosDocTop
SearchString("[- Hyphen][- Hyphen]")
ReplaceString("_")
ReplaceForward()
PosDocTop
CHAIN("mod_atrb.wpm")
```

Here's how to record it. Press Ctrl+F10, then type in *typeset* as the name of this macro. Now press Home, Home, Up arrow. Then press Alt+F2 and press the Space bar twice. Press Tab to move to the "replace" window, and press the Space bar once. Then press F2 to replace. Press Enter to get rid of the report window. Repeat this process: press Home, Home, Up arrow. Then press Alt+F2 and press the hyphen key twice, then press Tab. To enter the dash, press Ctrl+W, S, then use the arrow keys to select the typesetting symbols. Press C, then move down four rows and over three columns with the arrow keys to select the long dash. Press Enter. Press F2. Finally, press Home, Home, Up arrow. Now Press Ctrl+F10 to stop the recording.

Load the macro ("TYPESET.WPM") into Edit View from the disk, and on the bottom line type CHAIN("mod_atrb.wpm"). This will bring in WP's Replace Attributes macro. Now save your file again as *typeset.wpm*. It's ready for use.

This macro turns typewriting into typesetting.

One of WP's
most useful
built-in macros.

Note: WP includes several macros that were written by WP programmers, including the following:

Macro: MOD_ATRB.WPM

One of the most useful macros for desktop publishers is "MOD_ATRB.WPM," which allows you to search and replace such things as underlining and boldface. We "attached" this macro to our TYPESET.WPM macro by using the macro language command *CHAIN*.

Macro: Quick Exit

Some people find it annoying when they try to exit WP. WP displays some query boxes asking if you want to save the document, if you want to return to editing, if you really, truly want to leave. If you would prefer to immediately exit WP, no questions asked, type in this macro and save it under the name *exit.wpm*:

```
DISPLAY(Off!)
ExitWordPerfect
```

Now you can run this macro and it will send you right to DOS without any quizzes. Of course, if you want this fast exit to be truly fast, you'll want to create a key combination for it so you can just press, for example, Alt+E and you're outta there.

Now we'll look at how to make *keyboards* in WP. Keyboards allow you to assign key combinations to WP's built-in features or to your own custom features, your macros.

KEYBOARDS

With keyboards,
you can remap
the meaning of
your keys.

The idea of "keyboards" is that you can tell WP what you want it to do when you press Ctrl+*a key* or Alt+*a key combination*. (*Note:* You can also redefine the meaning of ordinary keys, such as *i* or *l*, but that would make it hard to type in text. If you don't use them often, though, the ~ (tilde), ` (accent) and [ ] (bracket) keys can be used as superfast ways to invoke macros or WP commands. You don't have to press

Ctrl+]; you can just hit the] key and the action takes place.) Many people find using [and] for a *delete word* macro makes editing go faster. Wherever your cursor is when you press [or], that word disappears (no blocking, no multiple presses of the Backspace or Delete key, just poof and it's gone). To do this, create a macro which deletes the word the cursor is on, then assign it in a keyboard to both the [and] keys.

Once a key combination is defined, instead of having to press Alt+F10 and then type in a macro's name, you can just press Alt+L, for example, and the lkern (left kern) macro does its job.

You can create as many keyboards as you like. WP saves them in the same directory as your macros, and it gives keyboards a file-name extension of .WPK.

Create as many keyboards as you want.

CREATING A KEYBOARD

To see how it works, let's put all the macros we created above into a new keyboard called MYMACS.WPK. Press Shift+F1 to get to the Setup menu. Then press 4, 2, and type in the name for the new keyboard: MYMACS. Press Enter and you'll see the Edit Keyboard window. Here's where you define the action WP should take when you press a key combination.

Press 1 (Create), then press the key combination for kern left (let's use Alt+L). Now press 5, 2, F6, and use the arrow keys to move down to Macros/Keyboards/Button Bars Personal, and press Enter. You'll see a list of all the WP-supplied macros, keyboards and button bars (and any you've created). Use an arrow key to move down to LKERN.WPM, then press Enter, Enter to put the Alt+L key combination assignment into the MYMACS.WPK personal keyboard.

Press 1 (Create) again and follow the same pattern to enter the following:

LKERN.WPM, RKERN.WPM, KERNON.WPM,
KERNOFF.WPM, ROTATE.WPM, TYPESET.WPM
and EXIT.WPM.

When you finish mapping your keyboard, exit the Edit Keyboard window (press F7). Then test the new keyboard: press 1 (Select) to make MYMACS the default keyboard.

Assigning Commands & Features to a Keyboard

Notice that when you're in the Edit Keyboard window, there are two options other than macros. You can assign key combinations to text (press 3) or commands (press 4). Using the text option, you could assign a key combination to some text that you want WP to type in whenever you press the combination. For example, if you often end letters with the sentence "Thank you for your cooperation in this matter," you could type in that text once (in the Edit Keyboard window) and forever after simply press Ctrl+E (or whatever keys you choose) to have WP type it in for you.

The other option, command, will show you a list of most WP features and behaviors—such things as indent, reveal codes, etc. You can directly assign one of these to a key combination (without having to create a macro for it).

BUTTON BARS

For mouse users, button bars can be a quick way to run a macro, a WP feature or a menu item. You can even add a button that brings up a different button bar.

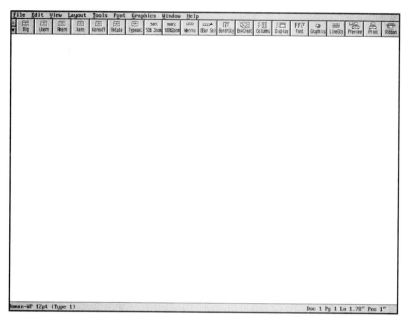

Figure 6-4: A button bar can extend across the entire Edit screen.

To create a personal button bar, press Alt+V, S, S, 2. Name this one *publish*. Then press 3, to add one of our macros to the button bar. Use an arrow key to select the name, then press Enter. Press 3 again to add the next macro, and so on, repeating until you've added all the macros you want on your button bar.

In this same window you can also add built-in WP features (press 2), add an item on a menu (press 1) or even add another button bar (press 4). If you run out of space, WP will darken one of the arrows in the upper left corner. Then a new bar will be started. This second bar can be accessed while you're writing or editing by clicking on the dark arrow.

It's simple to add to or create a button bar.

MOVING ON

In the next chapter we will look at some tools that are particularly useful for desktop publishers: how to get the most out of the Text and Image Editors, and how to insert and modify watermarks, borders, lines and captions.

Modifying Text & Graphics

7

The new WordPerfect features—including Graphics and Page Views—make desktop publishing much easier than it was in WP 5.1 and earlier versions. Before WP 6.0, you were largely confined to Text View for the creation of your documents. Needless to say, this required a lot of switching back and forth between viewing modes—when you imported a graphic or adjusted some spacing in Text View, you had to turn on Print Preview each time to see the results. In this chapter we'll explore these new, sophisticated features, such as the Image Editor, the Text Editor, watermarks, borders, lines and captions, that make it possible for you to do truly professional-quality desktop publishing.

THE NEW EDITING TOOLS

With WP 6.0, you can import, manipulate or create text and graphics, and see the results immediately and in a high-resolution visual environment. Some features are slower in Page or Graphics View, but there's no substitute for watching a change being made right before your eyes. Also, if you have a mouse, you can drag and resize boxes of text or graphics *dynamically.*

Choose from eight Graphics Box styles; each has a special purpose.

GRAPHICS BOXES

You can choose from eight kinds of Graphics Boxes: Figure, Table, Text, User, Equation, Button, Watermark and Inline Equation. You can put whatever contents you want into most any kind of Graphics Box. But the boxes differ from each other in two ways: each box type has its own particular default borders (although you can change the borders as you wish); and each box type offers different options (for example, when you create a Text Box, the Text Editor becomes one of the options).

In other words, WP knows which kind of box you're working with and provides the right tools to manipulate the contents it expects you to put into such a box. But there's one confusing aspect to all this: WP refers to any box (even if it contains text) as a Graphics Box. A box which typically contains a photo or drawing is called a *Figure Box*. But as a group they're referred to as the Graphics Boxes. I'm using WP's terminology in this book (but under protest) to avoid bewilderment. WP isn't the only company that sometimes causes unnecessary confusion by poor word choices. But why couldn't the general class of boxes have been called simply *Boxes*?

THE IMAGE EDITOR

The Image Editor lets you prepare a graphic image for insertion into a document.

While not a full photo-retouching program, such as Adobe's Photoshop or CorelPHOTO-PAINT, WP's editor does allow you to alter size, contrast and brightness and perform various manipulations such as inversions, vertical flipping and rotation. As you'll see, the Image Editor offers many ways to adjust and improve an image.

First, choose a picture and insert it into a Graphics Box (Alt+F9, 1, 1, 1, then type in the file name of the graphic image, or press F5 to use the File List windows). Press Enter twice to return to your document, then look at it in Graphics or Page View. You'll see something like Figure 7-1.

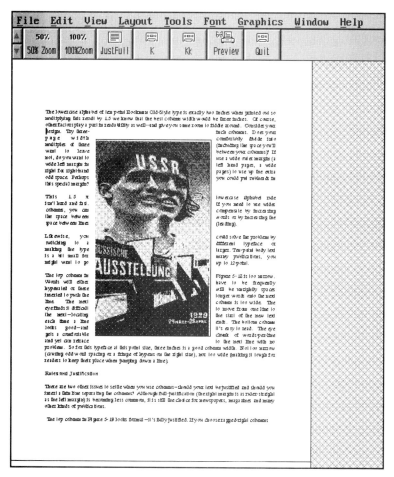

Figure 7-1: Viewing your graphic onscreen shows how it looks in relation to the rest of the page.

Take a look at your graphic. Would it be improved by increasing the contrast, enlarging a particular area (zooming in to remove the outer edges of the image), or by using some other technique available in the Image Editor?

Next you might want to print out a copy of the page to see how it will look in your finished document. Printers and monitors vary—what you see onscreen might not be exactly what you get when you print. (*Note:* when selecting Print options, always choose "High" graphics and text quality from the WP Print window. This way you'll get the best results your printer can deliver.)

To see precisely how a finished page will look, print a "proof."

Another way to check a photo or drawing is to zoom in to get a closer look, as in Figure 7-2.

Figure 7-2: Closer inspection shows that we need to create more contrast (the faces will be the center of attention). And it might also be a good idea to emphasize the highlights in the eyes.

Now go to the Image Editor. If the Graphics Box Edit window is still visible, press 3 to choose the Image Editor. If you're back in a document-editing view (Page, Text or Graphics View), press Alt+F9, 1, 2, Enter, 3. (If you have a mouse, just double-click on the image itself, then press 3.) Now your image is ready to be manipulated.

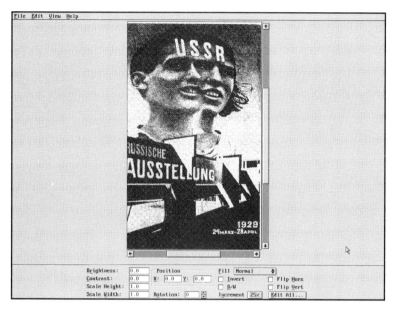

Figure 7-3: When you open the Image Editor, the full-sized graphic and a variety of options are displayed.

INCREASING CONTRAST

Depending on how you've set up WP, the Image Editor might display a button bar, a status box or merely a group of menus across the top. In Figure 7-3, the menus and status box are visible.

Let's experiment. Try turning up the contrast. You can press the period (.) or comma (,) key to decrease or increase contrast. Or press C to get into the contrast specification area of the status box. (If your status box isn't visible, press Alt+V, T.) Now you can type in a specific contrast value. –1.0 results in low contrast. We used 1.0 (high contrast) to get the effect in Figure 7-4.

Figure 7-4: High contrast brings out the lettering and the highlights of the eyes and teeth. For some printers, this will be the best choice. It's almost black-and-white.

High contrast creates powerful but less realistic images.

Notice how the USSR twins in Figure 7-4 look as if they have raccoon eyes now. The effect is like a hot light on the image. It turns the daylight effect seen in Figure 7-3 into a nighttime atmosphere.

High contrast reduces shadows, shading and most other gradations. In some ways, high-contrast images are the most powerful—though they're the least realistic. Increase contrast when you want to emphasize the graphic, when it is small, or if it is more of a design than a photographic representation (as is this poster).

If you have a mouse, you can use a WP-supplied button bar designed just for the Image Editor. Most of the tools in the Image Editor are available on the button bar. To bring it up, press Alt+V, B.

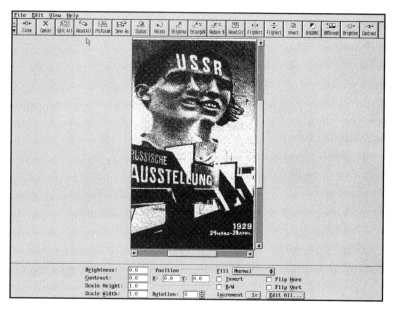

Figure 7-5: The button bar along the top is useful if you will be using a mouse.

If you don't like your changes, you can bring back the original by selecting Reset All. Either press Ctrl+Home or press Alt+E, R.

Figure 7-6: Here we've returned to the original contrast levels. It's never too late to undo changes if you're still in the Image Editor.

Now let's explore some of the other transformations available in the Image Editor. We'll bring in a different graphic.

ADJUSTING HEIGHT & WIDTH

You can independently adjust height and width. When you do, the original image, shown in Figure 7-7, becomes distorted, as seen in Figure 7-8. If you want to resize an image to give it a white frame around all four sides, change the width and height *by the same factor*. In Figure 7-8 we reduced the height by a factor of .3 but left the width alone.

Figure 7-7: This graphic has just been imported into the Image Editor. No changes have yet been made.

To change width or height, press G for height or W for width to get to the status box. Then type in the new width or height. Measurements are expressed as fractions of the originals. In other words, you'll see 1.0, which means the width or height is the same as the original. To reduce the height by one-half, type in .5 to replace the 1.0.

Another way to change width or height is by pressing E to get to the Edit All box. Then press 3, 3 to change the figure's measurements.

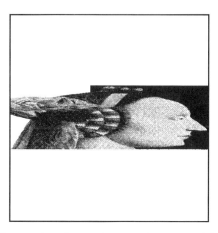

Figure 7-8: Reducing height without reducing width squeezes the image and distorts it.

SHRINKING A BOX

Notice that the Figure Box in Figure 7-8 has stayed the same size as the original. The *graphic* has shrunk, but the box has not. If you want to shrink the *box* along with the image, you'll have to do it in normal Page, Text or Graphics View. Here's how. First select the Graphics Box by pressing Alt+F9, 1, 2, Enter, 5, 1 (to get to Content Options). Now select 3, Preserve Image Width and Height Ratio and turn it off. Press Enter, Enter. Now WP won't try to retain the original shape of the graphic that you put into the box.

Back in normal document view (Text View), you can now specify the new width or height (or both). To do that, press Alt+F9, 1, 2, E, 9 to bring up the Graphics Box Size window. Then type in the new width or height.

You can do all this and more with a mouse. Drag the box by its "handles" (little black squares), click on the box and the handles will appear. Resize the box by pressing and holding the left mouse button as you move the mouse.

You can also move the image around within its Graphics Box. In Figure 7-9 we've moved the image –.02 to the left of its original X (horizontal) position. This adds white space inside the box on the right, without *cropping* (cutting off part of) the image. There *is* a way to crop images by enlarging them. We'll get to that later in this chapter.

Changing X and Y positions allows you to maneuver an image within its box.

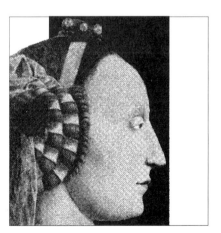

Figure 7-9: Changing the X position slides the image to the left within the box. Notice that part of the hair is no longer visible.

ROTATING AN IMAGE

One of the remarkable features of WordPerfect's Image Editor is its ability to rotate images any amount, from 1 degree to 359 degrees. This is something of a feat from a programming standpoint because rotation is a formidable task for a computer. What's more, the Image Editor rotates images relatively quickly.

Figure 7-10: Rotating 12 degrees creates an interesting effect.

Aside from the obvious visual interest you can add to a picture by rotating it, a slight off-axis rotation also adds a subtle impression of *motion*. If you compare Figure 7-10 to Figure 7-9, you may notice that the face in Figure 7-10 appears to be moving slightly backward, as if the woman is reacting to something she sees. This illusion can help to make your pages come alive (try rotating a picture of a bicycle or a car).

And it *is* an illusion—the eye compensates when the horizon line shifts. Ask yourself in which of these two figures the woman's head is being held precisely straight. In which figure is she looking directly ahead—neither up nor down? The answer is *both*.

Rotating an image makes it look like it's moving.

As an experiment, try loading in the drawing of floating balloons that WP supplies ("HOTAIR.WPG"). First try it straight, then see the difference when you tilt it 12 degrees or so. You should see the motion.

There's no ambiguity, however, when the rotation is extreme, as the 90 degree shift in Figure 7-11 demonstrates.

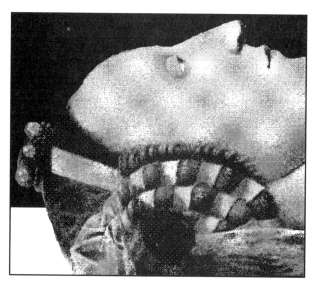

Figure 7-11: You can rotate an image up to 360 degrees.

INVERTING

Inversion, another transformation, creates a ghostly X-ray effect. Among other things, the eye now seems to be looking at the reader.

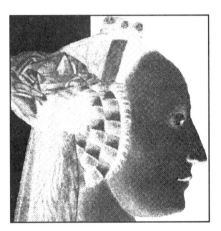

Figure 7-12: Inversion replaces all black dots with white dots and all white dots with black dots.

Selecting B/W (black-and-white) takes contrast to the maximum. This tactic is worth trying if your page needs some strong graphic punch, or if your paper or printer can't do a good job with grays. All shadow disappears, along with most texture and detail. But the result certainly stands out from the gray of body text.

Figure 7-13: The B/W setting reduces an image to its essentials.

FLIPPING

The Image Editor can also *flip* a graphic—horizontally or vertically. A picture can take on an entirely new character when flipped, as you can see in Figure 7-14. Recall that one of your design considerations is the *flow* of the lines on a page. You usually want strong lines flowing into the center of the page rather than out and off one of the sides. In this picture, the woman's nose forms an arrow shape; it's almost as directionally strong as a pointing finger. Therefore, if you're going to put this image on the right side of a page, you might want to flip it horizontally as in Figure 7-14. That way it will point the reader into the page. When flipping graphics, though, check for reversed words, backward watch or clock faces, a wedding ring on the wrong hand, and other embarrassing errors.

Figure 7-14: When flipped horizontally this image leads the eye strongly to the left.

THE INCREMENT OPTION

The *Increment* option on the status box controls how much effect pressing some of the shortcut keys will have on your image. You can adjust your graphic's brightness up or down by pressing < or >. Change its contrast via the , or . key. Enlarge or reduce it with the Page Up or Page Down key. Move the picture in all four directions with the arrow keys. The *increment* defaults to 10 percent, but you can press N and change the factor, which will cycle through 1, 5, 10 and 25. With an increment of 25, you'll make a 25 percent change with each keypress—your adjustments will be more drastic.

THE EDIT ALL WINDOW

Many of the options on the status box, button bar and menus at the top of the Image Editor are repeated in the Edit All window. Press E to bring up this window and you'll see that you can type in most of the same information. However, a few additional transformations are available only here in the Edit All window. To understand some of these special options, we'll have to digress briefly to explain the difference between *bitmapped* and *vector* images. WP can work with both types, and each has its strengths. But they are decidedly different kinds of images—both in the ways you can manipulate them and in the results you get when they are printed.

Use the Increment feature to govern how much effect the other features will have on your image.

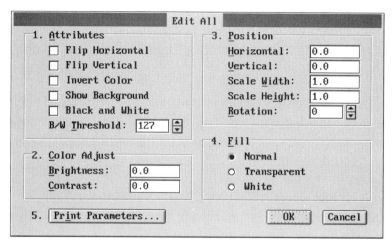

Figure 7-15: Some specialized adjustments to a graphic can be made only here in the Edit All window.

BITMAPPED VERSUS VECTOR IMAGES

Computers and printers can approach graphics in two ways: using an actual copy of the picture (a bitmapped image) or *describing* the picture mathematically (a vector image—giving circle horizontal location, vertical location, size, colors, fill patterns and so on). WP can work with both kinds of graphics.

Although there are dozens of minor variations in graphics formats, there is one primary division among formats. Images are stored, manipulated and printed by computers in two distinct ways: as bitmaps or as vector graphics.

A *bitmap* is a one-for-one "photocopy" of the original. Each dot of gray or color in the picture is stored in order in a disk file. On the other hand, a vector graphic *describes* the picture, and the picture is drawn on the fly when displayed or printed. A vector graphic is a set of mathematical notations about the position, size, shape, color and texture of the image, not a point-by-point copy. These two approaches apply to all computer graphics activity: bitmapped fonts—each in a single type size—versus scalable font languages such as TrueType and bitmap painting programs such as Paintbrush versus drawing programs like CorelDRAW.

Computers manipulate either a direct copy or a mathematical description of an image.

You can manipulate a bitmapped picture, such as a .TIF or .PCX file, by zooming in and adjusting any dot (pixel) in the picture. You may not need to work on that level; you can instead paint with a broad brush, fill whole areas or use a "spray paint" tool. But if you want to work on a particular dot, you can. And every dot will be stored on disk or sent to the printer.

Although this approach may seem wasteful of computer memory (a high-resolution full-screen image can take up as much as four million bytes, 4mb), it does make it somewhat easier for you to "paint" the images. It's also more intuitive because the screen becomes your canvas: you can use various tools (pens and brushes and so forth), and the closer you look, the more details you will see.

Working with a vector graphic in a program like CorelDRAW is radically different. You start by drawing a shape—by creating an area such as a circle or the shape of a face. The shape must be enclosed in order to be filled. Next, you can adjust the outer line (its thickness and color). Then you can adjust the fill (its texture and color). Finally, you can superimpose a new shape on top of an existing one, creating *layers*. This is how you would draw an eye shape on top of the face shape, a pupil shape onto the eye, a highlight on the pupil, and so on.

All the while, the program is creating a mathematical description of your shapes, textures and colors. The results are saved as a vector image (a mathematical description of the shapes and their locations, colors and textures). The .WPG files in WordPerfect are vector graphics, but the Image Editor can work with either vectors or bitmaps.

An important quality of vector graphics is that they can be enlarged without sacrificing any detail or becoming grainy. If you enlarge a bitmapped image, it will become increasingly coarse until, at the upper limit, you can see every *bit*. At that size, it will look like a mosaic. This is the same effect that causes you to see dots when you look closely at a picture printed in a newspaper.

Bitmapped images take up more room, on average.

Vector graphics can be expanded without losing detail.

The Many Minor Formats

There's a tower of Babel in computerland—each manufacturer seems to have developed its own graphics file format. CorelDRAW stores graphics in .CDR format, WordPerfect in .WPG format. Then there's PostScript (.EPS), .TIF, .GIF, .WMF, .BMP and others. Each format, however, will employ either the bitmap or the vector method of graphics storage.

WP will import some alien formats (.TIF, .PCX) but not others (.CDR or .EPS). Some shareware programs (such as PaintShop) and commercial programs (such as HiJaak and CorelDRAW) can translate between these formats. You could load a graphic in .TIF, for instance, and save it as a .PCX or .WPG. Programs such as CorelDRAW can load in most formats and save in most formats.

Not all graphics
formats are
accepted by WP.

SHOW BACKGROUND

This option in the Edit All window applies only to vector graphics. You'll see no effect if you're working with a .PCX or .TIF file, and perhaps none even with vector files. Show Background toggles any background patterns or colors which were included as options within a graphics file. You can try it, but most likely there will be no effect.

PRINT PARAMETERS

Press 5 in the Edit All window to see the choices (in the Image Print Parameters menu) shown in Figure 7-16.

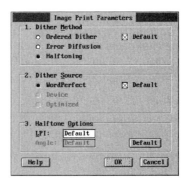

Figure 7-16: The specialized options in this window allow you to improve the appearance of an image—if your printer supports the options you want to use.

Dithering is an effort to produce relatively smooth gradations of gray (or colors). What's the problem? High-resolution is expensive. We've been watching low-resolution television (500 lines of light) since TV was first introduced to the consumer in 1953. Sometime before the millennium we'll probably get HDTV, high-definition TV (more than 1,000 lines).

The more lines, the more information is displayed (and the closer you can get to the image before it becomes grainy). The same principle applies to printed images and computer monitors. In some cases, images are reproduced as dots rather than lines. Newspapers use a system called *halftoning*: evenly spaced dots (of different sizes) are used to create the illusion of a continuous image with shades of gray. There *is* no gray, but at the distance you hold the newspaper from your eyes the dots blend into grays.

When the eye is far enough away (or if there are lots of dots creating *high resolution*), the brain won't notice the dots. The image will appear to blend from dark to light, or from color to color, in a natural way. Image resolution is often measured in DPI, dots per inch. Magazines typically have a higher DPI than newspapers—that's why magazine pictures look much more realistic. A picture in a magazine will have smooth gradations and display tiny details like eyelashes.

The figures we've used so far in this chapter have been reproduced via *ordered dither*. This oxymoron means that the dots are not lined up and equally spaced—instead there are patterns which more or less successfully indicate shading. Sometimes the patterns become too obvious and distracting, however. A face can look as if it's made of tweed.

A second dithering method choice in the Image Print Parameters menu is *error diffusion*, which eliminates repetitive patterns in favor of the somewhat wormy texture you can see in Figure 7-17. Here the shapes and the spacing are randomized—you don't see small patterns, but the overall texture, looked at up-close, is convoluted, like the surface of a brain.

Image resolution is measured in dots per inch.

Figure 7-17: Compare this error diffusion dither to the ordered dither technique used in Figure 7-7.

Halftoning is used for most newspaper graphics.

The final choice, *halftoning,* is common in newspapers, but you might not notice much difference between halftoning and ordered dither. When using halftoning, you can select the resolution by changing the LPI (lines per inch) density. You can also attempt to eliminate accidental patterns by adjusting the angle at which the lines are printed (this requires a PostScript-capable printer). If you attempt some of these adjustments, don't be surprised if you don't notice any difference. Printers capable of extremely high-resolution output are still expensive. Even most laser printers are capable of only 300 DPI. To get really sharp reproductions, you'd have to use about four times that density.

The Dither Source option on the Image Print Parameters window allows you to select whether WP or the printer will be responsible for describing the image to the printer. Some printers have capabilities beyond WP's built-in image description techniques. If Device can be selected (if it's not dimmed in the Image Print Parameters window), that means that you've told WP during setup that you have a PostScript-capable printer. Optimized means that your printer is capable of simulating greater resolution or otherwise smoothing text or graphics. The best way to decide if these options result in any improvement is to print some samples using each option.

VECTOR IMAGES

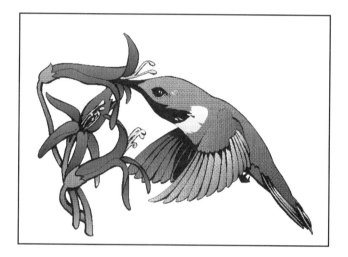

Figure 7-18: One of WP's supplied .WPG vector images.

Clearly, Figure 7-18 is a drawing, not a photograph. This is often the best way to tell whether you're dealing with a bitmap or a vector graphic. No matter how rough the texture or weak the detail, it's still obvious that Figure 7-17 originated as a photograph (of a painting). But, on the other hand, it's equally clear that Figure 7-18 originated as a set of superimposed shapes and colors that were *drawn*. Vector drawings, no matter how complex, always look somewhat like those elevation maps that show the contour of land—layers superimposed on layers.

Also, when you watch the Image Editor redraw a vector graphic, areas will appear to fill randomly as layers of shapes and colors are filled in and superimposed. It's like raindrops falling in slow motion onto a pond. A bitmapped graphic, by contrast, will seem to descend in an even line from the top—like a window shade being pulled down.

Vector graphics always look like drawings.

CROPPING

Sometimes you'll want to *crop* an image—that is, trim one or more of its sides. This can make your images more dramatic or effective by enlarging the essential elements and eliminating peripheral details. One way to do this is to move an image (press the arrow keys) until the main object you want to show is centered in the window. Then enlarge the image by pressing Page Up until you crop off the details you don't want to display.

Figure 7-19: You can crop an image by enlarging it. Here we've enlarged Figure 7-18 by 50 percent.

Enlarge Area

A second, similar way to crop is to use the Enlarge Area feature. The easiest way is to select EnlgArea on the button bar with a mouse, then drag the magnifying glass symbol to select the area.

You can do the same thing from the keyboard with a little more effort. Press Alt+E, P, A. Then use the arrow keys to position the magnifying glass. Press Enter and again use the arrow keys to move the glass to define the area. Press Enter when you're done.

Figure 7-20: Enlarge Area is another way to crop an image.

Notice in Figure 7-20 that we're not losing detail. In fact, we're now seeing details around the bird's eye that we couldn't see in Figure 7-19. This ability is limited to vector images. If you blew up a bitmapped graphic this much, it would look like a checkerboard—there would be no curves at this magnification, just stair-step shapes and squares. And there would be considerable roughness (*grain*) visible in the image.

Expand a vector graphic and you might see hidden details.

THRESHOLD

If you convert an image to black-and-white, you can control the results by specifying the B/W Threshold. Any grays (or shades of a color) below your threshold will turn black; those above the threshold will turn white. WP defaults to a value of 127 (right in the middle), but you can change the threshold to anything from 1 to 255. Press E to get into the Edit All window, then press 1 for Attributes and 6 to move to the B/W Threshold box.

Figure 7-21: A B/W Threshold of 60 creates a whiter image.

Figure 7-22: With B/W Threshold set to 160, the transformation results in a darker image; black predominates to create a near-silhouette effect.

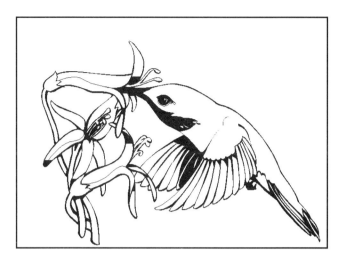

Figure 7-23: Set B/W Threshold to 50 and your image loses most of its shading and texture—a good way to emphasize the shapes and make the graphic look like a line drawing.

FILLS

The final option in the Image Editor is *Fill*, and it only works with vector graphics (not with bitmaps). You can select a transparent, white or normal (default) fill. Few images will respond to these changes other than to turn entirely white. But if an image has a distinct, separately described background, and fills that are subject to being rendered invisible, you can remove the fills as shown in Figure 7-24. *Normal* means the object "as is," unchanged. *Transparent* means the background, if any, will appear throughout because the fills have been removed from the foreground, leaving only the outlines of the object. *White* means that the fill will be replaced with solid white.

The fill option only works with vector graphics.

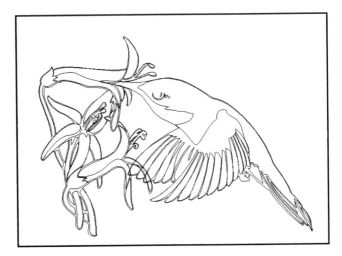

Figure 7-24: Selecting the White option for the fill removes all color and shading, leaving only the outlines of the vector graphic (the shape descriptions).

THE TEXT EDITOR

What's the point of a Text Editor when you've got a perfectly good word processor? The Text Editor can do most things you'd do in normal document-editing view (that is, create Graphics Boxes, type in headlines, change typefaces, and other such functions). However, the Text Editor is designed to allow you to edit text that has been placed into a Text Box. Also, in the Text Editor you can rotate and superimpose text. Those are its special tricks.

Figure 7-25: With the Text Editor, you can rotate text. And a Text Box can be superimposed on a Figure Box.

Beyond rotation, another virtue of placing text into a Text Box is that you can move the text around as a unit—placing it on the page exactly where you want it. And you can also superimpose the text onto a Figure Box or another type of box.

You can rotate, move or super-impose text by using Text Boxes.

Figure 7-26: Using the Text Editor is quite similar to using Page or Graphics View. You can even add a Figure Box within a Text Box.

To create a Text Box and get to the Text Editor, press Alt+F9, B, C, 3. You are now in the Text Editor, which, for all practical purposes, is like normal document view (but narrower). To rotate text, press Alt+F9, 5 while in the Text Editor. You can then select from 0, 90, 180 or 270 degrees of rotation. Press Enter after you've selected the rotation, then press F7 to close the Text Editor.

If you want to use the Text Editor to edit an already created Text Box, press Alt+F9, B, E, select the box number, press Enter, then press 3.

WATERMARKS

A Watermark Box in WP 6.0 is a special kind of Graphics Box; its specialty is superimposing. Put a picture or a headline or whatever you want into a Watermark Box, then move the watermark on top of something else. The contents of the Watermark Box will then appear *beneath* the body text or other elements of your document.

A Watermark Box is created like any other Graphics Box.

You create a Watermark Box as you would any other type of Graphics Box in WP. First, place your cursor at the point in the document where you want the watermark to appear, then press Alt+F9, B, C, 1. Select the file name of the image you want to use as the watermark (or press 3 for Create Text, and use the Text Editor to type in a text watermark). When finished, press F7 to exit the Text Editor (or press Enter to exit the file-name selection window). Now you should be back in the Edit Graphics Box window, and you can press Y (for Based on Box Style). At this point, select Watermark as your Graphics Box style.

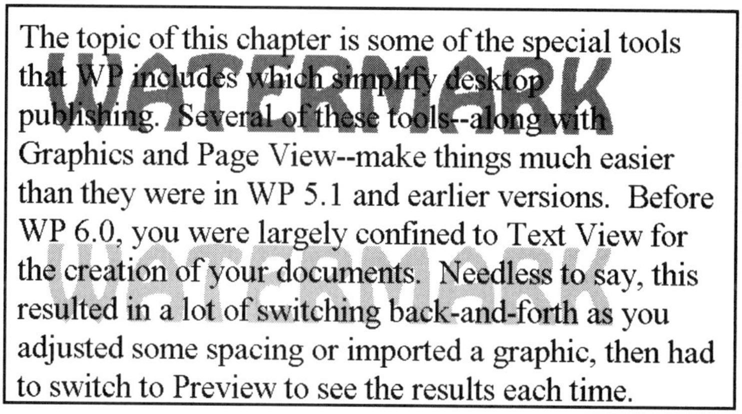

The topic of this chapter is some of the special tools that WP includes which simplify desktop publishing. Several of these tools--along with Graphics and Page View--make things much easier than they were in WP 5.1 and earlier versions. Before WP 6.0, you were largely confined to Text View for the creation of your documents. Needless to say, this resulted in a lot of switching back-and-forth as you adjusted some spacing or imported a graphic, then had to switch to Preview to see the results each time.

Figure 7-27: It's easier to read the superimposed body text over the lighter watermark on the bottom.

Because your watermark will usually be positioned underneath body text, you want to be sure that the body text remains readable. If the watermark is too dark, adjust the brightness. press Alt+F9, 1, 2, select the Box number, press E, 3, and you'll be in the Image Editor, where you can change the brightness. You'll see a figure such as 0.75, which means 75 percent white. (1.0 would be 100 percent white, and you wouldn't see *anything*.) Change it to perhaps 80 percent to make it slightly lighter, then test the results.

Note: Sometimes superimpositions, page frames, rotations and other special effects won't show up in Graphics or Page View when you return to your document from the Edit Graphics Box window. If that happens, select Print Preview or print out a copy to see how your page really looks. (Or you can temporarily switch to Text Mode, then back to Graphics Mode—to see if the screen redraw shows the results of your changes.)

You may not be able to see special effects when you switch back to an editing view.

BORDERS

A *Border* is similar to a *Box* in WP—you can select from built-in border styles, create a custom border style, etc. But a Border in WP is merely a visual effect enclosing a paragraph, column or page. A Box is a special feature of WP that allows you to move the contents around, resize the contents and otherwise manipulate the encapsulated graphics or text.

The topic of this chapter is some of the special tools that WP includes which simplify desktop publishing. Several of these tools--along with Graphics and Page View--make things much easier than they were in WP 5.1 and earlier versions. Before WP 6.0, you were largely confined to Text View for the creation of your documents. Needless to say, this resulted in a lot of switching back-and-forth as you adjusted some spacing or imported a graphic, then had to switch to Preview to see the results each time.

Now you can import or create text and graphics right in a high-resolution environment. Some of WP's features will be slower, but there's no substitute for being able to move something and see it move.
Also, you can drag and resize boxes of text or graphics dynamically if you have a mouse.

Figure 7-28: Borders can be used to segregate a special section of text from the rest of the body text.

To border a paragraph, put your cursor where you want the border to start, or block the desired paragraph(s) using Alt+F4, then press Alt+F9, O, P, 1, and you'll see the border styles displayed. The styles from which you can choose are None, Spacing Only (No Lines), Single, Double, Dashed, Dotted, Thick, Extra Thick, Thin Thick, Thick Thin, Thick Top and Bottom, Button, Column Border (Between Only) and Column Border (Outside and Between). Select a style by pressing S. (See Appendix A.)

Create column or page borders the same way. You can also specify a fill if you wish.

LINES (RULES)

There are two ways to insert lines into your documents: *Line Draw* and *Graphic Lines*. Line Draw is relatively crude when compared to Graphic Lines. Line Draw merely resorts to the old DOS-style character set, which has a limited number of line options and in many cases must compromise with dashes instead of solid lines. Contemporary printers can do far better than the relatively ineffectual lines that Line Draw permits. Moral: use Graphic Lines. Here's how: Put your cursor where you want the line, then press Alt+F9, 2, 1, 6, and choose the line style you want by highlighting it using an arrow key and pressing 1 to select it.

Avoid "Line Draw"; use the superior "Graphic Lines" instead.

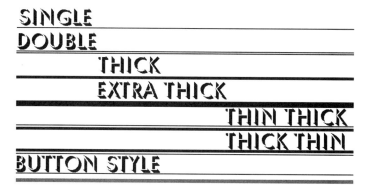

Figure 7-29: WP includes a variety of built-in line styles, or you can create your own.

There are many options when using Graphic Lines—color, thickness, spacing (relative to surrounding text), horizontal/vertical, etc. And, if none of WP's built-in line styles will suffice, you can create your own style and save it to disk for reuse. Press Alt+F9, 2, 1, 6, 2 to display the Create Line Style window. Then type in the file name you want to give to your new style. (You'll also find several levels of additional windows under this one.)

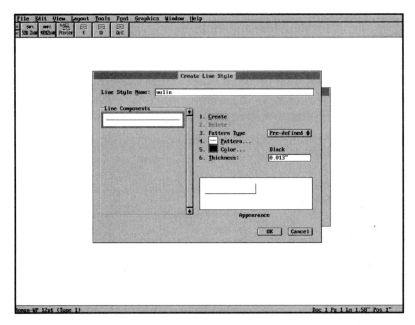

Figure 7-30: In this window choose pattern type, color and thickness for your own custom line design.

CAPTIONS

As you would expect, since it's generous in most respects, WP offers an exceptional array of facilities for customizing Graphics Box captions.

To access the caption options, press Alt+F9, B, E. Then select the number of the Graphics Box that you want to caption. Press 5, 2, and the Caption Options window will appear (see Figure 7-31).

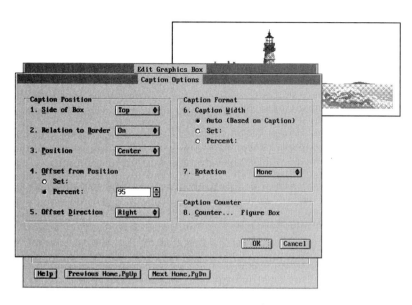

Figure 7-31: As you can see, in WordPerfect 6.0 there are many ways to manipulate captions.

Of the choices you have in the Caption Options window, the only potentially confusing ones are Offset From Position, Offset Direction and Caption Counter.

Offset From Position and Offset Direction allow you to be specific about the horizontal location of your caption. Once you've selected the gross position (for example, Center), you can nudge the caption a set amount or a percent amount (Offset From Position) away from that center. Offset Direction determines whether the Offset From Position goes to the right or to the left of, in this case, the center.

WP can help you with certain kinds of publications by automatically numbering items as you insert them into a document. *Caption Counter* can keep track by listing your Figure Boxes (Figure 1, Figure 2, etc.) as you add them. It can also renumber the figures should you delete or add some—thus maintaining the integrity of your numbering system.

Offsets allow you to precisely describe a caption's location.

MOVING ON

Next, we'll look at some before-and-after examples, called *makeovers* in the trade. The idea is that no design is ever awful or perfect. You can look at most any printed page and think of some alterations that could make it better.

Remember that there is no one right answer when you're designing something. Indeed, there are no 1,000 right answers. Style is highly subjective. Style is also ephemeral— what our grandparents thought was the cat's meow would seem to us cluttered, mannered, terribly conservative and generally off the mark.

Doubtless what appeals to our grandchildren will strike us as confusing, wild, rude, loud and unacceptable to decent people who know right from wrong. As far back as we have written records, the older generation has been responding to some of the styles of the younger generation with the comment, "I'm shocked. Shocked!"

The great thing about style, though, is that there *is* no right or wrong. The rules sound strict, but fashion shifts and flows like liquid.

One lesson that Van Gogh taught us is that often as people get older they close their eyes and minds to things new and unfamiliar, and they judge the present by the rules about beauty that they learned earlier in their lives. They are no longer willing to accept new styles. *We* can understand why a Van Gogh painting sells for $30 million, but in his time no one bought his work. What do we see that they did not?

So take the next chapter with a grain of salt. The suggestions are merely proposals based on current fashion and common sense. But in the end, do what looks good to you. You might even *start* a fashion by violating the "rules."

Good style can
be shocking.

Design to please
your own eye,
even if you break
some rules.

Before & After Designs

In this chapter we'll do *makeovers*—before-and-after designs —showing how common desktop publishing tasks can be successfully completed. Although you can profit by reading this chapter by itself, many of the principles and concepts we've used here are more fully explored earlier in the book. If you want to learn in greater depth about such things as *balance*, *appropriateness* and *design variety*, please see the index listings in the back of this book for references to these and other design techniques used in creating these examples.

In these makeovers, we'll examine how the *before* designs might be improved. Specific WP keystrokes are not included here, unless they demonstrate a technique not previously explained in Chapters 3 through 5.

We're going to be the desktop publishing artist for an imaginary financial planning company called Forward Finance Inc. We'll design company stationery, a fax form, a logo, an official report format, a flyer, a press release form, an in-house newsletter, a menu for the company restaurant and an advertisement that will appear in a magazine. The company wants to project a sober, thoughtful image—a corporate personality almost as conservative and reliable as a bank. But they also want the designs to be modern, sleek and, above all, *forward-looking* and *safe*.

We want to create a "sense of safety."

THE LOGO

We'll start with the logo since it will be used on the fax form and incorporated into other documents we'll do later. Logos are often built out of a distortion or symbolic adaptation of the company's initials, and that's what we're going to do here. We've got the initials FF to work with. Our first idea is to overlap the two letters, as shown in Figure 8-1.

Figure 8-1: BEFORE: This is our first try at a logo for Forward Financial Inc. The letters are too decorative.

Be sure that your choice of typeface is appropriate.

In our first attempt, the *idea* was a good one: suggest the "forward-looking" image by lifting the second F a little. Also, using italics naturally throws the letter shapes to the right (which is *forward*, since we read from left to right). But one of the problems with this design is that we selected a script ("fake handwriting") typeface. This fails the appropriateness test: script is only used these days for such things as printed invitations (weddings, anniversaries, etc.), lingerie ads, and restaurant menus and wine lists. Instead, we need a sans-serif block-like typeface such as the WP-Helve font used in Figure 8-2.

The second problem is that we've crowded the letters so close together that they are a tangle of lines and are hard to decipher. This doesn't say "modern" or "thoughtful"—it says "fancy but confused."

Figure 8-2: BEFORE: Not bad, but the "swastika" effect ruins it.

A FATAL FLAW

The second version, shown in Figure 8-2, has two problems.
The letters are again hard to decipher because they are still
too close together. However, this isn't a fatal flaw. Logos are
often so symbolic that they aren't recognized by the casual
reader until the logo becomes familiar through repeated advertisements. (Often you'll see the full name of a company set
in smaller type below the logo.) The fatal flaw in Figure 8-2 is
purely unintentional, but you've got to be alert to accidental
associations your design might create in the viewer's mind.
The design forms a swastika.

Figure 8-3: AFTER: Strength, solidity, readability.

Using the same typeface we used in Figure 8-2, we pull the
second F slightly to the right and down. This makes the letters
clearly readable as FF, and it also makes a pleasing design.

In WP, the easiest way to create a logo based on a company's initials is to use the Advance feature. Advance allows
you to position letters with great precision. Starting from
scratch, here's how to create Figure 8-3:

Select the typeface by pressing Ctrl+F8, F. Then use an
arrow key to select Helve-WP Bold and press Enter, S. Now
type in 42 as the type size and press Enter, Enter to get back
to document view.

Press Ctrl+I to select italics, and type in FF. Move the cursor between them—we're going to Advance the second F up.
To move the second F up, press Shift+F8, 7, 6, 4 to get to Advance Up From Cursor and type in .11 as the vertical lift.
Then press Enter, Enter, Enter, Enter and you'll see the same
results as in Figure 8-3.

Use WP's
"Advance"
feature to create
a logo out of
company initials.

TRIAL & ERROR

How did we know to type in .11 as the vertical movement? It's just hit or miss. Try a few different numbers until the logo looks right to you. Fortunately, the excellent viewing capabilities in WP 6.0 make this kind of experimentation easier than it used to be. Now save your logo to a disk file. We'll use it again for other documents we'll be producing.

THE FAX COVER

Most companies create a form to act as a fax "cover letter." This form gives the name, address and fax number of the sender, the time, the recipient's name and fax number, etc. Anything your company sends out to others represents your company—for better or worse. So you want to design a nice-looking, efficient fax form. In the case of Forward Financial Inc., the form should look serious and businesslike.

How does our design, shown in Figure 8-4, rate as a good design? It is a clean design, but there are a couple of thoughtless elements.

First, what does "FAX" under the "TO" mean? It is supposed to be the recipient's fax number, but we should make that clearer.

Second, "PAGES" is ambiguous because people won't know if the page count does or doesn't include the cover sheet. Finally, "COMMENTS" and the lines under it are not lined up with the left or right margin of other elements on the page.

As you can see in Figure 8-5, by extending the lines at the top to match the lines under "COMMENTS," we strengthen the symmetry of this page. Symmetry helps promote a feeling of security and balance.

Check the text in a document. Is everything clear, unambiguous?

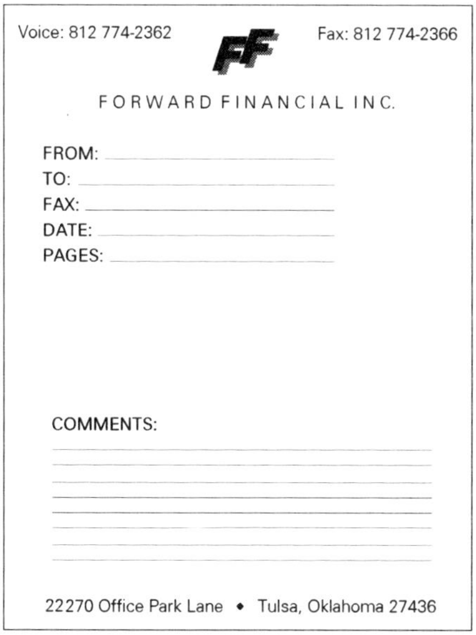

Voice: 812 774-2362 FF Fax: 812 774-2366

FORWARD FINANCIAL INC.

FROM: ______
TO: ______
FAX: ______
DATE: ______
PAGES: ______

COMMENTS:

22270 Office Park Lane • Tulsa, Oklahoma 27436

Figure 8-4: BEFORE: Nice and clean, but the page margins are not consistent and the piece isn't well balanced.

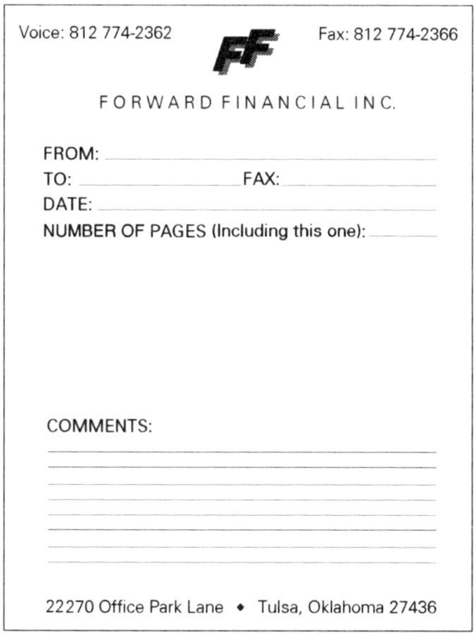

Voice: 812 774-2362 FF Fax: 812 774-2366

FORWARD FINANCIAL INC.

FROM: ______
TO: ______ FAX: ______
DATE: ______
NUMBER OF PAGES (Including this one): ______

COMMENTS:

22270 Office Park Lane • Tulsa, Oklahoma 27436

Figure 8-5: AFTER: Clarifying what "FAX" and "PAGES" mean makes the page more easily understood.

THE COMPANY STATIONERY

This project involves creating a design that will be used for the company letterhead—the first page of official correspondence. Subsequent pages will be blank. Like personal stationery, business stationery should endeavor to project the personality of the sender.

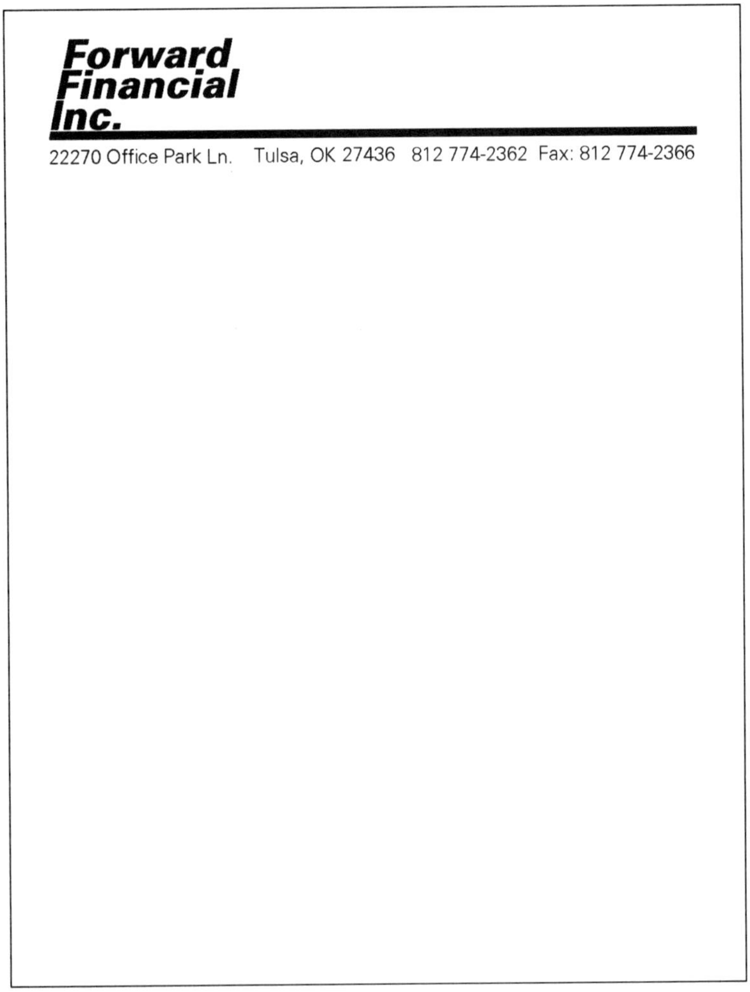

Figure 8-6: BEFORE: Not a bad design, but it moves the eye in the wrong direction.

ITALICS MOVE *FORWARD*

In Figure 8-6, the company name, Forward Financial Inc., looks good lined up this way—the first letters of each word positioned so they form a continuous angled line. All the letters are italics, leading the eye forward, as we want. However, the overall shape of the design forms a subtle arrow shape that points to the left. People read from left to right, so we're pointing them in the wrong direction, away from the contents of our page (see Figure 8-7). And we're working against what we want—a forward thrust to the right.

To reveal the shapes you've created on a page, draw lines around the graphics and text.

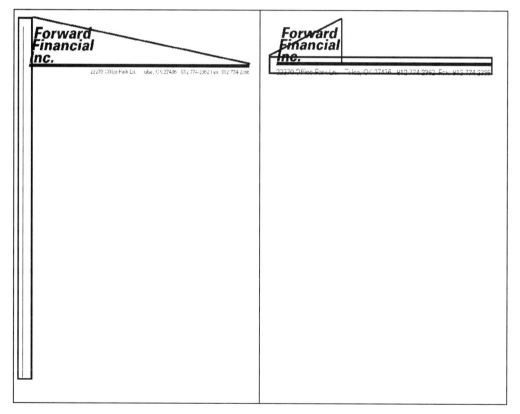

Figure 8-7: The shapes in your design are revealed if you draw lines around them.

The page in Figure 8-6 would be perfectly acceptable, but we can improve it by making the two adjustments shown in Figure 8-8. When we shorten the address and phone number and move them below the line, we add to the *rightwardness* of the shape. And a thin rule down the left side forms a boundary, a barrier, preventing the reader's eye from sliding off the page. The overall shape in Figure 8-8 now becomes flag-like and points primarily to the right.

Figure 8-8: AFTER: Now we're moving the reader *into* our document rather than out of it.

THE PRESS RELEASE

There are a few conventions when preparing a press release. One, a holdover from typewriter days, is the practice of setting the body text of the press release in the Courier (typewriter) typeface (as in Figure 8-10). At the top of the first page, you should include the date and the statement "For Immediate Release." Each page ends with --MORE-- except for the final page, which ends with a series of pound signs (# # # # # #). Also, the words PRESS RELEASE should be fairly large. Other than that, there are no hard-and-fast rules for designing a press release.

POSITIONING THE ELEMENTS

The most important consideration is how the reader's eye will scan the page. We decided to use elements of our company stationery but move the address, phone and fax info down to the bottom of the page.

Figure 8-9: BEFORE: The address is best placed out of the way at the bottom. Also, PRESS RELEASE needs to be kerned.

Kerning almost always improves headlines.

To reinforce the *forward* message we want to convey, and also to guide the reader into the document, we decided to move the title, PRESS RELEASE, below the main line. Then, putting the other *pro forma* "For Immediate Release" lines above, we created an arrow shape that points right. Also, because the lettering in Forward Financial Inc. is heavy, it nicely balances the extra text on the right side. We also kerned the letters to tighten up the letter spacing in the words PRESS RELEASE.

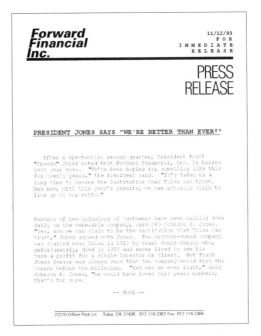

Figure 8-10: AFTER: Some repositioning makes this page stronger and less likely to be ignored or discarded.

THE ADVERTISEMENT

When you create an advertisement that will be placed in a newspaper or magazine, you're usually competing with lots of other ads. And most of their designers have the same idea: to catch the reader's eye.

MONEY & SIZE ARE POWERFUL ATTRACTORS

As discussed earlier in Chapter 2, you know you can attract readers with the human face or people in bathing suits, but other visuals work, too. Truly huge headlines or a photo of money, for instance. Money happens to be the business of Forward Financial, so we can use some coins or a stack of bills to get their attention.

Figure 8-11: BEFORE: The concept is good, but the contrast and positioning of the text could be stronger.

Consider the audience and the publication when designing an ad.

Another consideration is the nature of the audience you're trying to reach. The boss says he wants to get young adults with this ad, so the message in our design is bold, direct and a little slangy. (Compare this to the sedate proposal in Figure 8-16, which of course is directed to an older population.)

Also consider the context: where the ad will be published should have a direct bearing on the message and the "style."

The ad shown in Figure 8-12 is going into the sleek city magazine *Tulsa*, which is filled with jazzy Absolut vodka ads and other sophisticated designs. The same ad wouldn't work as well in an alumni newsletter or a religious publication. The text, WANT SOME, isn't excessively vulgar, but some might think it suggestive and maybe a little rude.

After we created the illustration shown in Figure 8-11, we realized that the space between WANT and SOME? should probably be substantially tightened (the larger the typeface, the narrower should be the distance between lines).

Also, the message packs more power if the words are not centered. Centering creates symmetry, and symmetry is a calm, settled look.

High contrast often works well in ads.

Finally, the 50 percent black of WANT SOME? is too close to the shade of the $20 bill. Without sufficient contrast, the text sinks into the money image, taking away from the realism of the stack of bills. (Lack of contrast often decreases realism—things look "painted on" each other and, thus, less real.)

To create a sense of dimensionality and to force readers to notice this piece, we decided to get as much contrast as possible. And nothing contrasts more than white-on-black. Most newspaper or magazine pages are white backgrounds with black interruptions. Our ad is black with white interruptions.

Figure 8-12: AFTER: White text on a black background is punchy and strong. It also creates a 3D illusion.

REVERSING TO WHITE-ON-BLACK

To create the look in Figure 8-12 using WP 6.0, first make the text white, large and bold. Press Ctrl+F8, C. Choose white as the character color, press Enter, then press F and choose a bold version of Helve or Univers. We used an even fatter typeface here: USA Black. WP doesn't supply this face, but you can add any typeface you want to WP's repertoire. (For instructions on adding typefaces, see "Font Installer" in your WP manual.) Next, select a large point size—we used 68-point. Then press Enter to return to normal document view.

Now we'll change the background to black. Press Alt+F9, O, A, F, and use the arrow keys to choose 100 percent black fill. Then press S to select it and press Enter to return to the document again. Now type in WANT SOME? and you should see white lettering on black.

Finally, we'll create a Graphics Box and allow the text to flow *through* the box so we can superimpose the word SOME? onto the image of the stack of $20 bills.

Earlier we used a scanner to make a copy of a $20 bill, folding the corner slightly to create a shadow. The scanner can pick up shadows, and this makes the bill look more realistic. Then in CorelPHOTO-PAINT we added a slight gray shadow around two sides of the bill to make it look like a stack. (You can just scan a real stack if you've got the cash.) Finally, we cropped off most of the image and saved it to a .PCX file that WP can read.

The next step is to press Alt+F9, B, C, T, F, and select Through Box so the text can be positioned on top of the image. Press 1 (Filename) and import the .PCX image of the $20 bill. Then press 7 and select Attach To Page so you can move the image into whatever position on the page you want. Use WP's Advance feature to position the words exactly where you want them. (*Note:* you won't see the superimposition of text over the image in Graphics or Page View—you'll have to print it out or select Print Preview to see the full effect.)

When you scan an image, try using shadows or other special effects.

THE MANUAL/BOOKLET

Whether for in-house use or for public distribution, your longer documents don't have to be boring. Too often a personnel manual, for example, will have a plain cover: just Courier lettering with the title in all-caps. It looks like something that was typed and photocopied instead of something that was typeset and printed. For a professional look, spend a few minutes adding some rules and maybe a screen, as we did in Figure 8-13.

Figure 8-13: BEFORE: Much better than the simple Courier typeface typically used on the covers of many corporate documents. But even this can be improved.

A SUGGESTION OF JAIL

After we came up with the design shown in Figure 8-13, we decided that it would look better if the vertical rules were closer together and were all the same width. (The vertical rules in the original design are slightly suggestive of cell bars, and we didn't want to risk a possible connotation of *imprisonment*.) Bringing the vertical lines together preserved the balance of this page but eliminated the unfortunate suggestion of jail. Adding a couple of boxes was a nice touch, and eliminating the unnecessary address information also improved the appearance (this is an in-house document—they know where they work). Finally, we removed the italic slant from Forward Financial because straight-up letters look better in this box.

Figure 8-14: AFTER: A lighter, less-threatening look.

THE BROCHURE/REPORT

A brochure is usually intended to describe a service or product to customers; a report is more often for in-house use only. Nonetheless, they both benefit from appropriate design.

Symmetry conveys conservatism.

The brochure shown in Figures 8-15 and 8-16 is targeted to a highly conservative group of senior citizens. We want the design to suggest solidity, dependability and security. Most people agree that the single most powerfully conservative design technique is symmetry. Figure 8-15 is largely symmetrical, but the main title, Retirement Opportunities . . . , is off-balance. It, too, should be centered.

We also want to choose a different typeface. This one isn't black enough and it isn't traditional. It's a noodly, round-edged, thin sans face. Also, the line spacing looks too loose. Finally, we'll add a couple of rules around the title, again suggesting safety and containment.

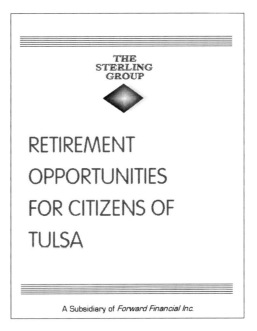

Figure 8-15: BEFORE: Conservative, but the main title needs work.

COMFORTING THE READER

By changing to the classic Roman face in Figure 8-16, we use the alphabet design common to bank documents, stock certificates and, indeed, money itself. A conventional serif face like this—even for a headline—comforts the reader and says, this company is not likely to do anything wild or experimental. Also, the smaller type size allows us to tighten the entire design—bringing both the logo, "The Sterling Group," and the "Subsidiary" information at the bottom closer to the center of the page.

The lettering of The Sterling Group title was done in a special "chiseled" typeface available in DeluxePaint (by Electronic Arts). We also used that excellent DOS-based graphics program to generate the highlighted diamond shape and its shadow. These elements were saved to disk as .PCX files then imported in WP into borderless Graphics Boxes. To be able to move them freely on the page, we selected Attach To Page in the Graphics Box editing window (press Alt+F9, 1, 1, 7, A).

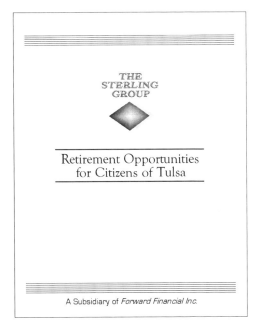

Figure 8-16: AFTER: A tight, traditional and highly symmetrical design conveys stability and reliability.

THE FLYER

A flyer is often a single page, folded in half or thirds vertically. It is an advertisement, like a brochure, but generally smaller in size. The flyer in Figure 8-17 is designed for the same audience as our brochure described above, but we're adding an extra come-on, Plan Now & Enjoy. . . . We're also rearranging the design elements to make them fit better on the narrower page. The page would be folded at the vertical line in the center.

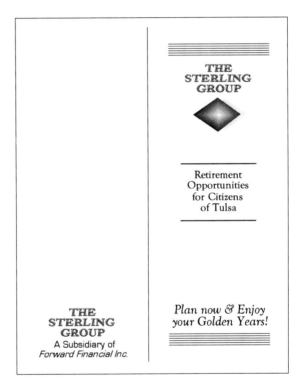

Figure 8-17: BEFORE: The front and back of a typical flyer.

A LITTLE TOO CAUTIOUS

Figure 8-17 can be improved by putting the main lure, Plan Now & Enjoy . . . , higher on the page and by adding a graphic. As is, this looks more like a stock certificate than an advertisement. We *do* want to remain conservative, but Figure 8-17 might be overdoing it a little.

How *do* you choose an appropriate graphic? One way is to make a list of the qualities you're trying to project. Then scan in a photo or select from some clip art—an image that most closely suggests those qualities. For this flyer, we looked at all the clip art supplied with WP. The concepts we want are *planning*, *enjoyment*, *foresight* and *old age*. We considered the hot air balloons and both skiers. The skiers seem too energetic for old age and don't look much like foresight either, flinging themselves, as they are, downslope.

The balloons are closer, but again the foresight element is weak—balloons drift on the wind with little control over their ultimate destination. The winner is the old sea captain with his hands on the wheel. The *enjoyment* factor is perhaps not obvious here, but for saying "solid control in old age," none of the others could beat this one.

Choose an image by first listing the qualities you want to convey.

Figure 8-18: AFTER: Enlarging the main message, removing 12 of the 14 horizontal rules and adding a graphic make this a more compelling design for a flyer.

THE DIAMOND MUST STAY

We were required to use that diamond logo (the boss insisted), but we put it on the back page to make room for the sea captain. We also got rid of most of the horizontal rules. That helped to lighten the page and take away the gray look. The lines were a dominating presence on the page but were of little value in getting the message across.

You might notice that, taken as a whole, Figure 8-18 is out of balance. The back page doesn't have the strength of the front page. But flyer covers aren't read full open, so your main concern is getting the right balance *within* each of these pages, not across the whole spread.

The covers of flyers are read as individual pages; the interior pages are read as spreads.

PLAN AHEAD & ENJOY!

■ Buy municipal bonds and don't worry about taxes for the rest of your life.

■ Eastern European or South American Funds offer 12-15% yields with virtually no risk until the 14th year.

■ Forward Financial Inc. provides monthly news on financial conditions free of charge.

■ Our Golden Retriever Money Market Fund is the leading financial instrument in Tulsa. For the past seven years, while other Tulsa-based funds have languished in the recession, the Sterling Group's no-load Golden Retriever Fund has shown an average annual return of over five percent.

22270 Office Park Ln. Tulsa, OK 27436
812 774-2362 Fax: 812 774-2366

Figure 8-19: BEFORE: Within the flyer lies the main message; if they've taken the bait on the front page, this is the hook.

The interior of a flyer *is* treated as a spread, and the pages that make up a spread should balance. They don't balance in Figure 8-19: we've got virtually no margins, and there is trapped white space (zones of blank paper) between zones of text. Also, the body text is rather large and, oddly enough, it's set in sans-serif type.

However, again we must design within constraints. We cannot change the type size or typeface—the boss wants it like this so that it will be "easy to read no matter how bad your eyes are." We'll have to work with what we've got. But we *can* make those bullets a little smaller so the pages have wider margins.

PLAN AHEAD

♦ Buy municipal bonds and don't worry about taxes for the rest of your life.

♦ Eastern European or South American Funds offer 12-15% yields with virtually no risk until the 14th year.

♦ Forward Financial Inc. provides monthly news on financial conditions free of charge.

& ENJOY!

♦ Our Golden Retriever Money Market Fund is the leading financial instrument in Tulsa. The past seven years, while other Tulsa-based funds have languished in the recession, the Sterling Group's no-load Golden Retriever Fund has shown an average annual return of over five percent.

22270 Office Park Ln. Tulsa, OK 27436
812 774-2362 Fax: 812 774-2366

Figure 8-20: AFTER: Our design is much improved now that we've filled the trapped white space.

REPEATING IMAGES

There's nothing wrong with repeating graphics. It adds continuity. And, in this case, it solves our trapped white space problem handily. We first reduced those overpowering bullets, making them small diamonds to echo the diamond logo. Then we added a little extra space to the margins around the body text. We had to change For the past seven years... to The past seven years.... But there's nothing wrong with that either. Then we forced & ENJOY! onto the same line by kerning ENJOY. Finally, we moved the blocks of text and the two imported graphics around until we got balance (so that these two pages will be easy to read as a unit).

NEWSLETTERS

Whether they're intended for internal or customer consumption, newsletters generally have three columns and less formal layouts than brochures or reports. Figure 8-21 is an in-house publication, so we should make it less official-looking—more relaxed and casual. (Even for a customer newsletter, Figure 8-21 is a bit on the gray side.) This calls for some photos or illustrations to break up the gray mass.

Figure 8-21: BEFORE: This design is OK, but modern readers are often put off by masses of gray text.

Fortunately, the company has recently offered for sale a commemorative coin—so we'll drop the illustration of the coin into the middle of the page. We can then also add some variety by putting a widely spaced caption under the coin. Making the Graphics Box that contains the coin slightly larger than the column text margins also helps to loosen things up.

The title, *Financial Times,* is set in a rather laid-back face called Bahamas. It's one of those tubular modern sans faces. However, the capital T in Figure 8-21 looks out of place because the design of the capital F is more like the lowercase f in most typefaces. We changed the T to lowercase. And the "Contents" box fill looked too dark at 50 percent black, so we reduced it to 25 percent black.

If a letter doesn't work, choose something else from the same typeface—or even design your own letter.

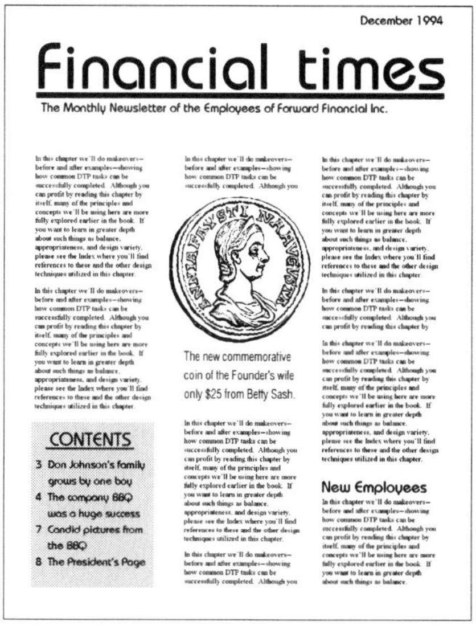

December 1994

Financial times

The Monthly Newsletter of the Employees of Forward Financial Inc.

In this chapter we'll do makeovers—before and after examples—showing how common DTP tasks can be successfully completed. Although you can profit by reading this chapter by itself, many of the principles and concepts we'll be using here are more fully explored earlier in the book. If you want to learn in greater depth about such things as balance, appropriateness, and design variety, please see the Index where you'll find references to these and the other design techniques utilized in this chapter.

In this chapter we'll do makeovers—before and after examples—showing how common DTP tasks can be successfully completed. Although you can profit by reading this chapter by itself, many of the principles and concepts we'll be using here are more fully explored earlier in the book. If you want to learn in greater depth about such things as balance, appropriateness, and design variety, please see the Index where you'll find references to these and the other design techniques utilized in this chapter.

CONTENTS

3 Don Johnson's family grows by one boy
4 The company BBQ was a huge success
7 Candid pictures from the BBQ
8 The President's Page

In this chapter we'll do makeovers—before and after examples—showing how common DTP tasks can be successfully completed. Although you

The new commemorative coin of the Founder's wife only $25 from Betty Sash.

In this chapter we'll do makeovers—before and after examples—showing how common DTP tasks can be successfully completed. Although you can profit by reading this chapter by itself, many of the principles and concepts we'll be using here are more fully explored earlier in the book. If you want to learn in greater depth about such things as balance, appropriateness, and design variety, please see the Index where you'll find references to these and the other design techniques utilized in this chapter.

In this chapter we'll do makeovers—before and after examples—showing how common DTP tasks can be successfully completed. Although you

In this chapter we'll do makeovers—before and after examples—showing how common DTP tasks can be successfully completed. Although you can profit by reading this chapter by itself, many of the principles and concepts we'll be using here are more fully explored earlier in the book. If you want to learn in greater depth about such things as balance, appropriateness, and design variety, please see the Index where you'll find references to these and the other design techniques utilized in this chapter.

In this chapter we'll do makeovers—before and after examples—showing how common DTP tasks can be successfully completed. Although you can profit by reading this chapter by

In this chapter we'll do makeovers—before and after examples—showing how common DTP tasks can be successfully completed. Although you can profit by reading this chapter by itself, many of the principles and concepts we'll be using here are more fully explored earlier in the book. If you want to learn in greater depth about such things as balance, appropriateness, and design variety, please see the Index where you'll find references to these and the other design techniques utilized in this chapter.

New Employees

In this chapter we'll do makeovers—before and after examples—showing how common DTP tasks can be successfully completed. Although you can profit by reading this chapter by itself, many of the principles and concepts we'll be using here are more fully explored earlier in the book. If you want to learn in greater depth about such things as balance.

Figure 8-22: AFTER: Adding a graphic and making a few other minor changes improves this page considerably. It's still not completely informal, but at least it seems more appealing.

THE MENU

Thanks in part to our successful designs and ads, Forward Financial Inc. is doing well enough to build a company restaurant—not a cafeteria, but a fancy French restaurant. And, of course, we've been asked to design the menu.

This is one of the few jobs where it's appropriate to use a script typeface. The format in Figure 8-23 is fairly straightforward, but the margins don't balance, and the little bullets are too close to the text. Also, the *ij* combination in *Bijou* creates a distraction with that double dot; but such effects are not generally considered serious flaws because script typefaces are decorative and eccentric by nature and must be judged on a different level. Nonetheless, the menu lacks character, personality, interest. It doesn't *say* anything graphically.

Aside from the rather obvious adjustment needed to the margins, our main problem here is that the design is boring and plain. The *lettering* certainly isn't simple, but the overall composition doesn't have strength—it's just a list.

A design can be so simple that it lacks personality.

Figure 8-23: BEFORE: Aside from the too-narrow left margin, this is a workable, if bland, menu.

After adjusting the spacing of bullets and margins, we enlarged the type size of the letters in The Chef Suggests from 14 points to 20 points. (As a general rule, you don't want headlines too close in type size to the body text they accompany.) Next, by adding page borders, we give the whole design more depth. It now looks something like a brass plate—more solid, more durable, than a simple piece of paper.

THE SNAKE EYES PROBLEM

The next step was to do something about those double dots that were still the focus of the whole page—your attention goes right to the "snake eyes." We solved the problem by putting *other* dots on the page—tacking one in each corner and, as a side benefit, amplifying the brass plate look. Now that they've got some company, the double dots don't attract as much attention.

To add a border to a page, press Alt+F9, O, A. Then select the style you want (or create a new one of your own). For Figure 8-24, we selected WP's thick-thin style.

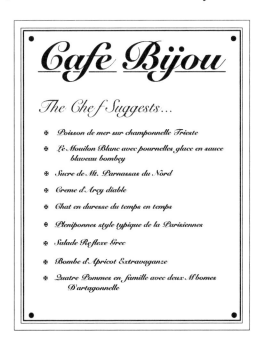

Figure 8-24: AFTER: Adding a page frame and some large dots gives this menu some personality.

MOVING ON—
WHERE TO GO FROM HERE

As you may have noticed, there are lots of theories about "proper" design: which typeface best serves a particular purpose, which designs create which moods and so on. However, I've tried to stress in this book that such theories should, at most, be considered guidelines.

No book can give you *the* complete, definitive list of design rules, though some try. And even if there were such a book, it would be quickly out of date. Design, like the other arts, is constantly revising itself.

Perhaps the most helpful tactic—if you want to continue to become a more effective desktop publisher—is to look at the best in current publications. Study page layouts, graphics and typeface choices, etc., in well-designed magazines such as *Vanity Fair, Esquire, Details* and *Interview*. Or if you have a specific publishing job coming up, such as designing a company logo or company stationery, look at other companies' logos or stationery. Find examples that appeal to you, then look closely at the elements of these good designs to find out what makes them so good. You don't want to copy these successful designs, but you do want to be educated and inspired by them. Since there really are no rules, you'll have to rely on your own educated eye. It's my hope that this book contributes, in some measure, to that education.

Borders & Typefaces

When you want to surround an illustration or a section of text with a box, you can press Alt+F9, 1, 1, 6, 1, and select one of the built-in styles.

MAKING BOXES & BORDERS

WordPerfect 6.0 ships with the set of ten predefined box styles shown in Figure A-1. If you want to separate sections of a page with horizontal or vertical lines, you can press Alt+F9, 2, 3, and you'll see an almost identical list of predefined line styles. The only difference is that there is no Thick Top & Bottom option—you have to create that yourself. To do that with lines, you would insert two Thick lines into your page. The predefined line styles also include the two halves of the Button style (Button Top Left and Button Bottom Right).

PARAGRAPH BORDERS

WP also includes a facility for adding a border to a paragraph, column or the entire page. You add a border by pressing Alt+F9, 3, 4. The border styles are also identical to those shown in Figure A-1, except there are two additional styles for columns: Between, and Between & Around.

DESIGNING YOUR OWN LINE STYLES

And don't forget that if one of the built-in styles isn't what you want, you can always design your own box, line and border styles. To create a new line style, for example, press Alt+F9, 2, 1, 6, 2, and type in the name of your new style.

Then press 3 and select Custom. At this point you can specify the length of dots and dashes within the line, choose color and thickness, and even add other variations to the style—for example, you can create double-line styles like the Thick Thin built-in style. Then you can save your custom styles to disk for future use.

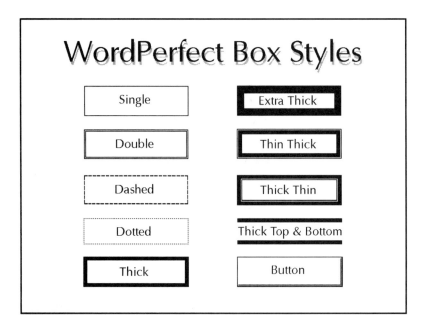

Figure A-1: WordPerfect offers a variety of built-in styles for lines, boxes and borders.

BUILT-IN TYPEFACES

WP 6.0 comes with seven basic typefaces: Bodoni, Commercial Script, Courier, Dutch (Roman), Helve-WP, Roman-WP and Swiss. The Hewlett-Packard LaserJet printer supplies CG Times, Courier, Line Printer and Univers. Your printer will have at least one, probably several, built-in typefaces.

PRINTER TYPEFACES

During the Setup procedure, when you tell WP the name of your printer, WP adds the printer's built-in fonts to the fonts that come with the WordPerfect program. To reveal the combined list of built-in printer fonts and WordPerfect fonts, press Ctrl+F8, 1.

Figure A-2: Some of these fonts are supplied with WordPerfect 6.0; some are built into the Hewlett-Packard LaserJet printer.

In addition to the seven typefaces supplied with WP and those built into your printer, you can add other typefaces to WP. (See Chapter 3.)

Resource List

Listed below are the products I have used in my own work and can personally recommend to enhance and amplify WordPerfect's desktop publishing capabilities.

COMPUTER-GENERATED ART

As yet unmatched in quality and capabilities, DeluxePaint makes it easy to create computer-art backgrounds and graphics. If you enjoy the balls-floating-in-space type of graphic or a surreal-looking landscape, you'll like this program—it can generate this kind of thing quickly and easily.

DeluxePaint® Animation
DeluxePaint™ Enhanced for IBM
Electronic Arts
P.O. Box 7578
San Mateo, CA 94403
(415) 572-2787

TYPEFACES, CLIP ART & DRAWING

Whether you want to create bitmapped or vector graphic illustrations, backgrounds, fills, borders or whatever, no competing software includes all the features of CorelDRAW.

The new version of CorelDRAW (Version 4) includes over 750 high-quality typefaces. Clip art is a collection of illustrations that you can import into your WP documents. CorelDRAW includes over 18,000 individual drawings.

CorelDRAW!
Corel Systems Corp.
1600 Carling Ave.
Ottawa, Ontario K1Z8R7
(613) 728-8200

IMAGE RETOUCHING & MANIPULATION

Adobe's Photoshop and CorelPHOTO-PAINT both do an excellent job of allowing you to adjust contrast, clone areas, smear, sharpen, diffuse and otherwise improve graphic images. Adobe also features color correction and 4-color separation. However, CorelPHOTO-PAINT is included in the CorelDRAW package, so you get a drawing program, hundreds of typefaces, thousands of pieces of clip art, a graphics database and much more in one purchase.

CorelPHOTO-PAINT
Corel Systems Corp.
1600 Carling Ave.
Ottawa, Ontario K1Z8R7
(613) 728-8200

Adobe Photoshop
Adobe Systems
1585 Charleston Rd.
Mountain View CA 94039
(800) 833-6687

PRINTERS

If you can afford it, a laser printer is superior to any other kind currently available. Now that Hewlett-Packard has introduced a model costing less than $1,000, you might want to consider laser technology rather than alternatives such as inkjet or dot-matrix—both of which have lower resolution.

Hewlett-Packard LaserJet printer
Hewlett-Packard
3000 Hanover St.
Palo Alto, CA 94304
(415) 857-1501

Many of the Hewlett-Packard LaserJet-compatible clones are solid and reliable. Check computer magazines for repair track records, current discount prices and print quality. Most laser printers use the same printing engine, so the differences between them, if any, are slight.

SCANNERS

There are several high-quality yet inexpensive hand-scanners. Among the best-known are the Logitec scanners. If you intend to include graphics in your desktop publishing, the Logitec Scanman Model 256 is a good choice. It can make good copies of drawings and photos in books, magazines or any other flat source.

Scanman 256
Logitec, Inc.
6505 Kaiser Dr.
Fremont, CA 94555
(415) 795-8500

DESKTOP PUBLISHING
WordPerfect 6

To **install**, insert disk in drive A: (or B:) and type install.

Companion Disks Sneak Preview

Expand your WordPerfect 6.0 desktop publishing capabilities with the valuable tools in this two-disk set! The disks include art shown in the book that you can import into your own Word-Perfect documents, plus dozens of useful macros and other prewritten timesavers, including

- A full set of 29 macros.

- A redefined keyboard, which makes activating the macros only a keystroke away.

- A specialized DTP button bar featuring several macros and a suite of WP's built-in desktop publishing facilities.

- Shortcuts for instant rotation and kerning—no more complex menu-surfing.

- Simple, easy-to-follow instructions showing you how to customize the macros, including a personal address book, a personal word & phrase list, instant insertion of frequently used special characters (like the copyright symbol) and more.

The powerful set of tools on this set of disks will amplify your desktop publishing capabilities and help you achieve your design goals quickly and effectively. If you're not completely satisfied, your money will be returned.

Glossary

A

Alignment
How text is justified: Flush-left (aligned on the left margin, with ragged right margin); flush-right (aligned on the right, with ragged left margin); centered (each line positioned around a center axis); fully justified (left and right sides align with the respective margin).

Attributes
The qualities of a typeface—italic, bold, etc.

B

Bars
Lines (or rules) which separate text. Thick lines are often referred to as bars.

Baseline
If you drew a horizontal rule under the letters in a line of text (those that do not have descending strokes, such as p and q), that would be the baseline.

C

Caption

A line or two of text underneath a photo or drawing, describing the image.

Clip art

Predrawn graphic images packaged with retouching, drawing, word processing or other software programs (or sold as self-contained products). Clip art is used to illustrate your publications. WordPerfect comes with several clip-art images. CorelDRAW! comes with thousands. You can import these files (use Retrieve Image, Alt+G, R) into your documents instead of drawing a picture yourself.

Continued line

See Jumpline.

Contrast

The degree of black versus white. A high-contrast image is mostly blacks and whites, with few if any grays. A low-contrast image looks mostly gray. A silhouette is very high in contrast. A photograph usually has medium contrast (the full range from black to white, through many gradations). A watercolor or pastel has low contrast (with little black and many gray shades).

Copy

The words or text of an article. The writer's output.

Crop

To crop means to trim. You lop off part of an edge (or edges) of a drawing or photo. This is usually done so that the essential element of the image is given more focus. Cropping gets rid of unnecessary peripheral details.

Cursor

A highlighted line or block on your computer's video screen which shows your current position within text or graphics where the next thing you type will appear or the next action you take will show up.

D

Default

A "standard" setting (for typeface, margins, etc.) that WP will use unless you tell it otherwise. Each time you fire up WP, it will *default* to certain conditions. Change the defaults by pressing Shift+F1 and choosing your options.

Dingbat

A small graphic image. Dingbats are used as "bullets" to introduce a list of items or point the reader to something—a small hand with a pointing finger is a dingbat.

Dithering

Strange patterns that occur when a printer or video screen attempts to simulate some in-between shades of gray or color. Since WP allows you to choose 100 shades of gray, some of them will fall outside the range of smooth reproduction if your printer is limited to producing 64 or fewer shades. (You need not worry about this if your printer can produce 256 or more shades of gray.)

Downloadable fonts

Also called *soft fonts*, these are typefaces you can send to your printer's memory when you first start up WordPerfect, or to have available as choices in the Fonts menu.

Drop

A larger (deeper) than normal margin at the top of a page. (Also called a *sink*.)

Drop cap

Also called *initial cap* or *display cap*, this is a capital letter set in a type size much larger than the type used in the body text. It is often used to introduce a new section of text.

Drop shadow

A shadow effect used with text or graphics.

E

Ellipsis

Three dots within a sentence (or four dots to end a sentence) that represent text that's been omitted or to indicate a break in continuity.

Em dash

A dash that sets off a group of words within a sentence. It acts like a set of commas or parentheses, but it makes a stronger break with the preceding and following text. Dashes can be used for emphasis, stress or to signal a digression.

Em space

A space equivalent to an em dash. *See* Em dash.

En dash

A dash half the size of, and sometimes substituted for, an em dash.

F

Folio

The date, issue number and volume number of a publication. Also, the page number.

Font

See Typeface.

Footer

The companion to *header*. A footer is a line of text at the bottom of a page in a multipage document or book. It can include the title of a chapter and the page number.

Formatting

Specifications for page setup, such as type size, margin size, line length and leading.

G

Greeking

Using "nonwords" to simulate the gray masses of text that will later be replaced by actual text in the final phase of publishing. Using greeking lets you evaluate and alter type size, column width, line spacing and other page elements in relation to the text blocks.

Gutter

The white space between columns of text. *Gutter* can also mean the space between two facing pages in a document or book—the place where the pages of the publication are fastened together. Make your gutters wide enough to allow the reader to easily *retrace* (*see* Retracing).

H–I

Hyphen

The short dash character that connects two or more words together to form compound modifiers. In the German language, and Welsh, words tend to coagulate. *Head Postmaster* might become something like *Headpostmasterhauptfuhrer.* A hyphen is also used at the end of a line of text where a word should be broken into its component syllables.

Initial cap

First used centuries ago as a decorative touch, initial caps are still used to add variety or balance to page design. Initial caps can also provide the reader with signposts to mark divisions between sections or zones of your publication. *See also* Drop cap and Chapter 4.

J–K

Jumpline (or "Continued line")

A line in a newspaper or magazine that tells the reader to *jump* to a new page to continue reading the article. Annoying, but helpful in selling advertisements or getting more stories toward the front of the publication, since advertisers assume that readers are more receptive when they start reading. It can also permit more stories on the front page of a newsletter.

Justification

Where a line of text is positioned in relation to its left and right margins. *See* Alignment.

Kerning

Pulling pairs of letters closer together to improve the appearance, particularly in a headline. *See also* Chapter 3.

L

Landscape

The orientation of a page printed across the length, rather than the width, of 8¹⁄₂" x 11" paper. When you select landscape (from the Print Menu), your page will be printed 11" wide x 8¹⁄₂" long. *See also* Portrait.

Laser printer

A printer that utilizes the same technology as copier machines—sending out a blast of heat in the shape of your text or graphics then releasing a quick fog of black ink onto the hot paper.

Current laser printers average 300 DPI (dots per inch), but if you want to spend about $1,200 more you can go up over 1,000 DPI (as good as it gets in the publishing world).

Other types of printers (inkjet, dot matrix) can approximate the output of a laser printer. But if you look closely, the curves of letters and the diagonals or dots within an illustration are rough and somewhat crude compared to those produced by a laser printer.

Leading

Adding space between lines of text. Unless you specify the amount of *lead* you want, the distance between lines of text is determined automatically by the *point size* (type size, *which see*) you have selected.

Letter spacing

The amount of space between letters, numbers and other characters in the text. WP's default letter spacing for body text is usually quite good and readable. But headlines are a different story; there is often too much space. In headlines you will almost always want to tighten the space between some letter pairs. *See also* Kerning.

Logo

A symbol that represents a company. A company logo is often a stylized rendition of the company's initials combined with other graphic elements. *See* Chapter 8.

M–N–O

Macro
If you repeat a series of keystrokes or functions (like going through a series of submenus to change the spacing between letters), you can *record* and name your actions and make them into a macro. Forever after, you can just invoke the macro by name instead of executing the whole sequence of steps to accomplish the goal. *See* Chapter 6.

Masthead
In a magazine or newspaper, a listing of the publication's staff members—publisher, artists, designers, editors, writers, etc. Also may include the address of the publication and other pertinent information. This listing is usually enclosed with borders that form a box.

Newspaper columns
In a newspaper-style column, the text is read from the bottom of one column to the top of the next column. *See also* Parallel columns.

Orphan
A short line (usually one or two words) at the top of a page or column. Orphans are distracting. *See also* Widow.

P

Paragraph spacing
The distance between the last line in a paragraph and the first line in the paragraph that follows.

Parallel columns
The text can be read horizontally *and* vertically—like a TV script. *See also* Newspaper columns.

PCL (Printer Command Language)
A page description language (graphics file type .PCL) invented by Hewlett Packard. It is a set of rules defining how computers should store and reproduce graphics.

Pixel
The smallest item of data on a TV screen or computer monitor. One of the "dots" you can usually see if you get close enough to a TV. The number of pixels on a screen determines *resolution*—the capacity to show detail. Computer monitors usually have higher (better) resolution than ordinary TV sets. *See also* Resolution.

Portrait
The orientation of a page printed the normal way: the page is read across the $8\frac{1}{2}$" width, like ordinary business letters. When you select portrait orientation (from the Print Menu), your page will be printed $8\frac{1}{2}$" wide x 11" long. Portrait orientation is used for most documents.

PostScript
A page description language (graphics file type .EPS, which stands for Encapsulated PostScript) developed by Adobe. PostScript files tend to be huge (4mb isn't uncommon), but they can be compressed using such programs as PKZIP, available on most bulletin boards. .EPS and .TIF files are the two most popular graphics file formats among graphic artists and production departments.

Proof
A "hard" (paper) copy printout of a computer file. When you print a copy of a page or document to see how it will look on paper, that's a *proof*.

Pull-Quote
A sentence or two taken from the text, usually set in boldface, larger than the body text. Pull-quotes are supposed to attract the reader to the story or article.

R

Raised cap
See Initial cap; Drop cap.

Resident font
A typeface that's "resident," that is, built into a printer when you buy it. Almost all contemporary printers include at least one resident sans typeface (like Helvetica) and one resident serif typeface (like Times Roman).

Resolution
The quantity and quality of detail you can see in an illustration. Image resolution is often measured in DPI (dots per inch). Magazine illustrations typically have more DPI than newspapers. They are much more realistic, with smooth gradations and clear details.

Retracing
Moving the eye from the end of one line to the start of the next line. Retracing is difficult if a column is too wide.

Reverse
Printing an illustration or headline with a black background and a white foreground. A strong effect, but it should be used sparingly.

Rotation
Changing the angle of text or graphics. Rotation is what happens when you put your finger in the middle of a photo on your desk, then revolve the photo around the center. WP can rotate text 90 degrees (making it vertical rather than horizontal), 180 degrees (turning it upside down) or any other increment up to 360 degrees in a circle.

Rule
A line. Rules are used to separate headlines from body text, to separate one column from another and to set off page elements such as pull-quotes.

S

Sans-Serif type

Typefaces designed without *serifs*, without the little extra jots and curlicues at the ends of the strokes. Sans-serif characters are more modern-looking. They are usually preferred for headlines.

Scaling

Resizing an illustration.

Scanner

A computer peripheral (costing anywhere from $100 to $5,000) that runs a light over a slide, photograph, magazine page—even your arm (anything flat enough)—then turns the scanned object into a graphics file on the computer's disk. This file can then be manipulated in WP's Image Editor (or with a photo-retouching program like CorelPHOTO-PAINT). Likewise, the file can be imported into a WP Graphics Box.

Screen

A block of gray used under (or behind) text or graphics as a background to make them stand out more on a page. Create a screen by selecting a fill for a WP Text Box (press Alt+F9), then select None for that box's border style.

Serif

See Sans-Serif.

Sidebar

A short section of text related but supplementary to the main article. Sidebar text is usually put into a box. Both magazines and newspapers are using sidebars more and more these days.

Sink
See Drop.

Small caps
Capital letters set 20 percent to 25 percent smaller than the capital letters used in the surrounding normal body text. Select Small Caps via Ctrl+F8, 3, 7—it's a typeface "attribute" in WP (like boldface or underlining).

Soft font
A typeface kept on the computer's disk that can be loaded into a printer as needed. Soft fonts can expand and enhance your library of typefaces.

Spread
Two pages designed to be viewed and read as a unit. You want to design facing pages so that they balance each other and work together harmoniously.

Styles
Close cousins to macros but more versatile for some kinds of tasks. Styles are best for formatting large documents that you might need to change or reuse in the future. If a document will be a *template* for future documents (such as a quarterly report), format it with styles.

T

Table
A grid of information, like a spreadsheet. (It can be read both horizontally and vertically.)

Template
See Styles.

Thumbnail sketch

A tiny representation of a page, a graphic or an individual design feature. Some software programs (such as Corel's MOSAIC) let you build thumbnails and show a dozen or so together, in a small size, on your computer screen. You could also print out small thumbnail versions on your printer.

Tint

A shade of gray or a color. In WP, you can adjust the shade of a Graphics Box's shadow by pressing Alt+F9, 1, 6, 5, 2. Then you can select the *amount* of black. If you choose a tint other than 100 percent black, you should select 75 percent, 50 percent or 25 percent, to avoid dithering effects. *See* Dithering.

Tracking

Changing letter spacing. Unlike *kerning*, which changes the space between two characters, letter-spacing changes in WP can affect more than a single pair of letters at a time. *See also* Kerning; Chapter 3.

Typeface

A specific version, or design, of the letters of the alphabet. Included in a typeface's character set are uppercase and lowercase letters, numbers, punctuation marks, and sometimes small caps and symbols.

Type size

Type size is normally measured in printer's *points* (abbreviated pt.). There are 72 points in an inch; each point measures .0138 of an inch. Because of their designs, certain typefaces appear smaller even in *the same type size* compared to some other typefaces.

Type style

See Attributes.

W

Widow

A short line (one or two words) at the end of a page or column. A widow leaves an awkward gap in the text. *See also* Orphan.

Word spacing

The distance between words. To adjust word spacing in WP until it suits you, press Shift+F8, 7, 9, 6. *See also* **Kerning; Letter spacing.**

Wraparound

Text flowing around an illustration. The text lines are automatically adjusted by WP so that they contour around the shape of a graphic. WP calls this "text flow" and allows you to select several kinds of wraparound for a Graphics Box by pressing Alt+F9, 1, 2, 1. Enter the box to edit and Enter, T, 1.

Index

Colophon

Desktop Publishing With WordPerfect 6 was produced on a Macintosh Quadra 950, a Quadra 700 and a IIcx using PageMaker 4.2. Screen captures were acquired with Hijaak for Windows, and scanned graphics were acquired with a Hewlett-Packard ScanJet IIc, using Ofoto scanning software. The cover was created using QuarkXPress 3.2 and Adobe Photoshop.

Body text is set in Adobe Palatino. Heads and captions are Adobe Optima.

Page proofs were printed on a Hewlett-Packard LaserJet III and an Apple LaserWriter IIg. Final film output was produced on a Linotronic L330 imagesetter.

the
Ventana Press

Desktop Design Series

To order these and other Ventana Press titles, use the form in the back of this book or contact your local bookstore or computer store. Full money-back guarantee!

Return Order form to:
Ventana Press, P.O. Box 2468, Chapel Hill, NC 27515
☎**919/942-0220; Fax 919/942-1140**

Can't wait? Call toll-free, 800/743-5369

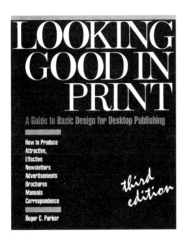

Newsletters From the Desktop
$23.95
306 pages, illustrated
ISBN: 0-940087-40-5
Now the millions of desktop publishers who produce newsletters can learn how to dramatically improve the design of their publications.

The Makeover Book: 101 Design Solutions for Desktop Publishing
$17.95
282 pages, illustrated
ISBN: 0-940087-20-0
"Before-and-after" desktop publishing examples demonstrate how basic design versions can dramatically improve a document.

Type From the Desktop
$23.95
290 pages, illustrated
ISBN: 0-940087-45-6
Learn the basics of designing with type from a desktop publisher's perspective. For use with any hardware or software.

Looking Good in Print, Third Edition
$24.95
424 pages, illustrated
ISBN: 1-56604-047-7
With over 200,000 copies in print, **Looking Good in Print** is looking even better, with a new chapter on working with color, plus sections on photography and scanning. For use with any software or hardware, this desktop design bible has become the standard among novice and experienced desktop publishers alike.

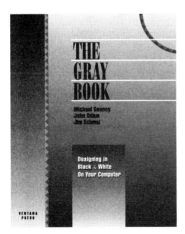

The Presentation Design Book, Second Edition
$24.95
258 pages, illustrated
ISBN: 0-940087-37-5
How to design effective, attractive slides, overheads, graphs, diagrams, handouts and screen shows with your desktop computer.

The Gray Book
$22.95
208 pages, illustrated
ISBN: 0-940087-50-2
This "idea gallery" for desktop publishers offers a lavish variety of the most interesting black, white and gray graphics effects that can be achieved with laser printers, scanners and high-resolution output devices.

Two Invaluable Ventana Guides

The Official America Online Membership Kit & Tour Guide puts the world at your fingertips—AT NO RISK! You'll find everything you need to take full advantage of this exciting online service, including

♦ The America Online starter disk.

♦ 10 FREE hours of online time for new & current members—a **$30.00 value!**

♦ Your America Online *Tour Guide*, a readable, richly illustrated "traveling companion" to help you get the most from your time online.

Novice and experienced online users alike will find *The Official America Online Membership Kit & Tour Guide* an exciting, value-packed alternative to the slower command-structured services.

The Official America Online
Membership Kit & Tour Guide
Tom Lichty
ISBN: 1-56604-025-6
$34.95   391 pages

Save time and money and increase your productivity with this unique, three-in-one guide! Completely revised and expanded to include information on the latest versions of DOS (6.0), WordPerfect (6.0) and Lotus (2.4), *DOS, WordPerfect & Lotus Office Companion, Third Edition*, written for beginner as well as veteran users, offers hundreds of tips, techniques and lots of practical advice for getting the most from your business software.

YOUR BUSINESS SOFTWARE Over 150,000 in Print!

DOS, WordPerfect & Lotus
Office Companion,
Third Edition
Patrick Burns
ISBN: 1-56604-048-5
$21.95   400 pages

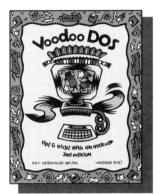

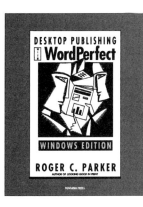

TO ORDER additional copies of *Desktop Publishing With WordPerfect 6* or any other Ventana Press title, please fill out this order form and return it to us for quick shipment.

	Quantity		Price		Total
Desktop Publishing With WordPerfect 6	_____	x	$24.95	=	$_____
Newsletters From the Desktop	_____	x	$23.95	=	$_____
The Makeover Book	_____	x	$17.95	=	$_____
Type From the Desktop	_____	x	$23.95	=	$_____
Looking Good in Print, Third Edition	_____	x	$24.95	=	$_____
The Presentation Design Book, Second Edition	_____	x	$24.95	=	$_____
The Gray Book	_____	x	$22.95	=	$_____
Desktop Publishing With WordPerfect Windows Edition	_____	x	$21.95	=	$_____
Desktop Publishing With WordPerfect 5.0 & 5.1	_____	x	$21.95	=	$_____
Desktop Publishing With Word for Windows	_____	x	$21.95	=	$_____
DOS, WordPerfect & Lotus Office Companion, Third Edition	_____	x	$21.95	=	$_____
The Official America Online Membership Kit & Tour Guide: PC Edition	_____	x	$34.95	=	$_____
Voodoo DOS, Second Edition	_____	x	$21.95	=	$_____
Voodoo WordPerfect for Windows	_____	x	$19.95	=	$_____

Shipping: Please add $4.50/1st book for standard shipping, $1.35/book thereafter;
$8.25/book for "two-day air," $2.25/book thereafter.
For Canada, add $6.50/book. $_____

Send C.O.D. (add $4.50 to shipping charges) $_____
North Carolina residents add 6% sales tax $_____

                                               Total $_____

Name _____ Co. _____

Address (No PO Box) _____

City _____ State _____ Zip _____

Daytime telephone _____

____ VISA ____ MC Acc't # _____

Exp. Date _____ Interbank # _____

Signature _____

Please return to:
Ventana Press, PO Box 2468, Chapel Hill, NC 27515 919/942-0220; FAX: 919/942-1140
CAN'T WAIT? CALL TOLL-FREE 800/743-5369 (orders only)

TO ORDER additional copies of *Desktop Publishing With WordPerfect 6* or any other Ventana Press title, please fill out this order form and return it to us for quick shipment.

	Quantity		Price		Total
Desktop Publishing With WordPerfect 6	_____	x	$24.95	=	$_____
Newsletters From the Desktop	_____	x	$23.95	=	$_____
The Makeover Book	_____	x	$17.95	=	$_____
Type From the Desktop	_____	x	$23.95	=	$_____
Looking Good in Print, Third Edition	_____	x	$24.95	=	$_____
The Presentation Design Book, Second Edition	_____	x	$24.95	=	$_____
The Gray Book	_____	x	$22.95	=	$_____
Desktop Publishing With WordPerfect Windows Edition	_____	x	$21.95	=	$_____
Desktop Publishing With WordPerfect 5.0 & 5.1	_____	x	$21.95	=	$_____
Desktop Publishing With Word for Windows	_____	x	$21.95	=	$_____
DOS, WordPerfect & Lotus Office Companion, Third Edition	_____	x	$21.95	=	$_____
The Official America Online Membership Kit & Tour Guide: PC Edition	_____	x	$34.95	=	$_____
Voodoo DOS, Second Edition	_____	x	$21.95	=	$_____
Voodoo WordPerfect for Windows	_____	x	$19.95	=	$_____

Shipping: Please add $4.50/1st book for standard shipping, $1.35/book thereafter;
$8.25/book for "two-day air," $2.25/book thereafter.
For Canada, add $6.50/book. $_____

Send C.O.D. (add $4.50 to shipping charges) $_____
North Carolina residents add 6% sales tax $_____

                                                                    Total $_____

Name _____ Co. _____

Address (No PO Box) _____

City _____ State _____ Zip _____

Daytime telephone _____

____ VISA ____ MC Acc't # _____

Exp. Date _____ Interbank # _____

Signature _____

Please return to:
Ventana Press, PO Box 2468, Chapel Hill, NC 27515 919/942-0220; FAX: 919/942-1140
CAN'T WAIT? CALL TOLL-FREE 800/743-5369 (orders only)

NOTES

NOTES

NOTES

NOTES

NOTES

NOTES

NOTES

NOTES